MISSOURI PACIFIC

PASSENGER TRAINS

THE POSTWAR YEARS

PATRICK C. DORIN

TLC
PUBLISHING INC.

2003
TLC Publishing, Inc.
1387 Winding Creek Lane
Lynchburg, Virginia 24503-3776

International Standard Book Number   1-883089-71-9
Library of Congress Catalog Card Number   2002101138

Design and production by
Kevin J. Holland
type&DESIGN
Burlington, Ontario

Produced on the MacOS™

Printed by
Walsworth Publishing Company
Marceline, Missouri 64658

OTHER BOOKS BY PATRICK C. DORIN FROM TLC –

The Challenger
Chicago & North Western Freight Trains and Equipment
Chicago & North Western Passenger Service – The Postwar Years
Chicago & North Western Passenger Equipment
Louisville & Nashville Passenger Trains – The Pan-American Era (with Charles Castner and Bob Chapman)
Louisville & Nashville – The Old Reliable (with Charles Castner and Ron Flanary)
Michigan – Ontario Iron Ore Railroads
Minnesota – Ontario Iron Ore Railroads
Missouri Pacific Freight Trains and Equipment
Western Pacific Locomotives and Cars

FRONT COVER AND TITLE PAGE –

Dome passengers survey the scene as the northbound *Texas Eagle* pauses at Austin, Texas, in August 1964. (J. Parker Lamb)

FRONTISPIECE –

Stainless steel eagles were a hallmark of Missouri Pacific's passenger diesels. (Electro-Motive, Kevin J. Holland Collection)

Dedicated to the memory of

Camille Chapuis

He provided a great deal of inspiration and encouragement for the creation of this book as well as other projects on the Missouri Pacific.

Camille was an extraordinary individual who is missed by many, not only for his knowledge of railroad operations, but most of all for his friendship.

THE AUTHOR

Patrick C. Dorin has been interested in railroads since the age of two.

While attending undergraduate school at Northland College, he worked for the Great Northern Railway. Later he worked for the Elgin, Joliet & Eastern Railway, the Duluth, Missabe & Iron Range, and the Milwaukee Road. His employment in the railroad industry included positions in operations, marketing research, customer service, and cost accounting.

He holds degrees in business administration, marketing, elementary education, and school administration including a Ph.D. from the University of Minnesota.

He recently retired as a school principal for the Superior, Wisconsin, schools and has taught marketing, operations research, transportation, Japanese culture, and school administration courses on a part-time basis for both the University of Wisconsin–Superior and the University of Minnesota–Duluth.

Railroads continue to hold a strong fascination for Pat, and he has published over 30 books and nearly 30 articles on aspects of railroad service, companies, and equipment, as well as other subjects.

Pat Dorin lives in Superior, Wisconsin, with his wife Karen.

ACKNOWLEDGMENTS

This book began as a single volume on the Missouri Pacific Railroad. As time went on, it became obvious that it was really a two-book project (the first, *Missouri Pacific Freight Trains and Equipment*, was published by TLC in 2000). The project would have been literally impossible were it not for a number of people who provided a great deal of their time and energies to assist the author. A giant thank you to everyone for their kind assistance.

My wife Karen put up with many inconveniences during the rewriting stages and provided much assistance by reading and checking the manuscript as well as reviewing various proofs.

A number of people from the Missouri Pacific were most enthusiastic about the project, including Mr. Harry Hammer, Assistant Vice President, Mr. Walter Fussner, Director Special Projects, Mr. D.M. Tutko, Chief Mechanical Officer, and many other staff members in the operating, mechanical, and public relations departments.

Members of the Missouri Pacific Railroad Historical Society also were extremely helpful. Mr. Ralph Barger and Mr. Jim Bennett both assisted with photography, news items, and the passenger car equipment rosters and diagrams.

Mr. Tom Dixon of TLC Publishing lent his insights and organizational suggestions for reshaping the original manuscript. Editorial assistance was provided by Mr. Kevin J. Holland, who also designed and assembled the book and obtained images from several sources.

A special note of thanks must go to Mr. Jim Perske for the amount of time he spent in the lab working with photographs for use in the book. The same is true for Mr. Dennis Roos, who assisted the author by traveling to Kansas to complete photography as well as contacting other sources.

The many photographers included Messrs. Ron Merrick, Camille Chapuis, Harold K. Vollrath, George C. Corey, A. Robert Johnson, W.C. Whittaker, A.C. Phelps, R.J. Wilhelm, W.S. Kuba, J.W. Swanberg, Bob Lorenz, R.H. Carlson, Bill Pollard, Elmer Treloar, Howard S. Patrick, Tom Dorin, J. Parker Lamb, Lou Schmitz, William Raia, H.E. Williams, and Scott Huch.

Harry Stegmaier, John Aenslic, Julian Barnard, and Jay Williams allowed the use of photographs from their respective collections.

Ms. Coi Gehrig of the Denver Public Library's Western History Collection gave permission to publish views from the Otto Perry Collection.

Additional research assistance came from Mr. Luther Miller, Editor of *Railway Age*; Mr. William J. Trezise of the National Railway Publication Company; and Mr. Michael Burlaga.

Without the kind assistance of these organizations and individuals, this book simply could not have been completed.

Should an acknowledgment have been inadvertently omitted, the author trusts that it will be found in the appropriate credit line within the text.

Thank you again—each and every one of you.

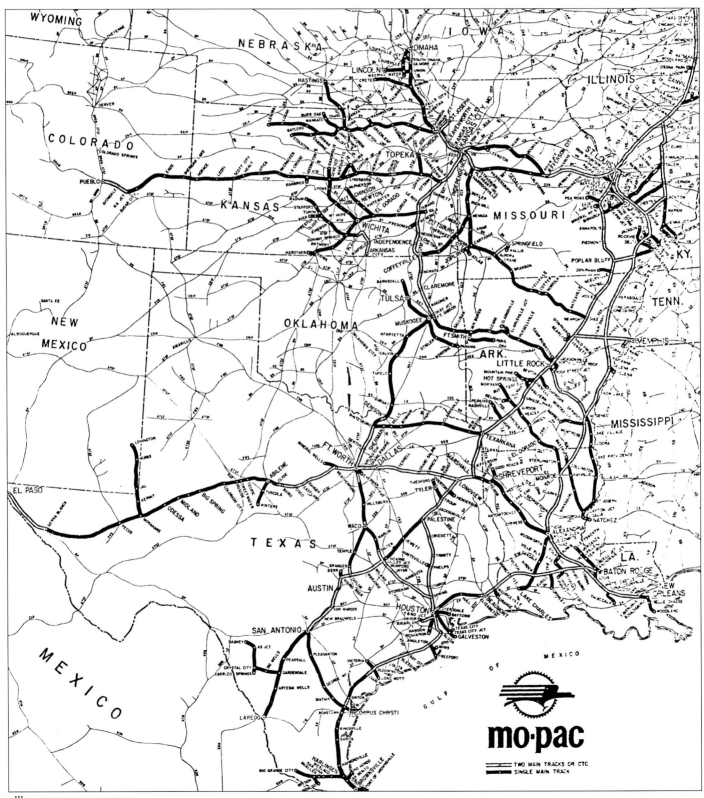

mo·pac

TWO MAIN TRACKS OR CTC
SINGLE MAIN TRACK

INTRODUCTION

The Missouri Pacific ("MoPac") and its subsidiaries operated a varied fleet of passenger trains throughout the territory south and west of St. Louis, Missouri, the company headquarters. The famous *Eagle* streamliners were only part of the fleet that could be seen, ridden, and otherwise enjoyed by travelers, shippers, and rail enthusiasts alike. At their peak, MoPac's passenger trains extended from Chicago to Mexico City, and from the eastern seaboard to Texas by way of interline connections. Commuter trains were in operation in the St. Louis area. Add in the mail trains, especially with their intermodal operations, and one has a railroad passenger operation with a great deal of variety and potential.

This book is structured into two major sections, covering train services and passenger equipment. The passenger equipment section (Chapters 7 through 11) includes representative photos, diagrams, and roster summaries providing both sets of number series (before and after the 1963 renumbering).

Chapter 5 takes the form of a color portfolio, informally dividing the book's two sections and presenting a variety of trains, equipment, and timetable advertisements for one of the nation's extraordinary railroads—the Missouri Pacific Lines, route of the *Eagles*.

Patrick C. Dorin
Superior, Wisconsin
January 15, 2003

CONTENTS

Bound for Memphis,
Missouri Pacific train
No. 220 leaves Little
Rock, Arkansas,
behind E3s 7000-7001
in June 1960.
(J. Parker Lamb)

A BIT OF HISTORY

When one stops to think about it, the Missouri Pacific Railroad operated the largest passenger service west and south of Chicago, *without* having a single through passenger train to or from the Windy City. Granted, there were through cars operated between Chicago and Hot Springs, and even Chicago–Mexico City, but not a single MoPac through train.

Many railroads—including the Great Northern, Northern Pacific, Union Pacific, Southern Pacific, Rio Grande, and Western Pacific—participated in through-train services to and from Chicago. Without such through operation, one can wonder how it was that the MoPac provided such an extensive train service, especially in view of its prolonged bankruptcy and a whole host of other problems.

The Missouri Pacific Railroad was not considered to be a front runner among railroads in the

1930s or 1940s by any stretch of the imagination. Few could have predicted 60 years ago that the MoPac would ultimately become one of the United States' leading transportation companies. If one observed the changes and improvements in passenger service beginning in 1940, however, it would have been obvious that things were taking place that would transform the entire character of the Missouri Pacific, a character that would demonstrate a foremost positive attitude, not only in passenger service, but in freight service and other areas as well.

Slipping back to the 1930s, the MP map was blanketed with a variety of trains, mostly locals, but also the famous *Sunshine Special* inaugurated in December 1915. The year 1940 marked the debut of the new *Eagle* streamliner fleet which was to play a major role in the total MoPac and T&P passenger services until Amtrak day in 1971.

World War II suspended much of the MoPac's efforts to expand, streamline, and improve passenger services. There was simply too much work to do. However, the *Colorado Eagle* did go into service in 1942, and the company doubled passenger service between Denver and St. Louis. It was double-daily in each direction with the Rio Grande participating in through-train services between Pueblo (the MoPac's western terminal) and Denver.

Rail service was not the only area to be improved, even during the war. In 1942, MP purchased six new buses for Missouri Pacific Trailways. The new buses were of 37-passenger capacity, completely air-conditioned, and were operated on schedules in Louisiana. At the time, MoPac Trailways owned and operated 148 buses. It is interesting to note that the MoPac was an early believer in "multimodal" passenger services.

Pacific-type (4-6-2) No. 6503 led a two-car local on March 2, 1933, (Lou Schmitz Collection)

3

This St. Louis, Iron Mountain & Southern Railroad passenger train's portrait was taken in 1890, location unknown. Ten-wheeler No. 643 heads up one wooden head-end car and four open-end coaches. Note the link and pin coupling device on the "cow catcher," and the wooden station platform. (Missouri Pacific, Author's Collection)

MoPac was severely taxed during the war, but was able to handle its share of troop movements with a great deal of efficiency—and effectiveness. When equipment was short, the company would use the *Missouri River Eagle* equipment for a fast round-trip movement between St. Louis and Kansas City during the night, and still have it ready for the daylight run the next day. The com-

pany was always looking for ways to keep ahead of the situation.

Missouri Pacific also attempted to launch an airline service known as Eagle Airlines. Despite much fanfare, however, it never got off the ground, and the name "Eagle" was instead maintained with great success in the railroad's growing fleet of streamliners.

Another facet of MoPac passenger trains was the self-propelled "gas-electric" car, operated on scores of branch lines throughout the system. The company used both full head-end service and combination mail/baggage and coach styles of equipment. (Missouri Pacific, Author's Collection)

above: MoPac gas-electric coach No. 626 with trailer No. 1003 (an RPO-Baggage car) at Centralia, Illinois, on the Missouri-Illinois Railroad in June 1939. This equipment ran on M-I trains 1 and 2 between Salem and Flinton, Ill., daily except Sunday. In 1941, No. 1 departed Salem at 8:50 a.m. and arrived at Flinton at 11:57 a.m. The equipment then laid over for 65 minutes, departing Flinton at 1:02 p.m. with an arrival of 4:45 p.m. at Salem for the 78.4-mile run.

middle: Another example of gas-electric equipment was No. 650, a combination coach and baggage car photographed at Lincoln, Neb., on June 11, 1954, by Carl Hehl. (Both, Lou Schmitz Collection)

bottom: Missouri Pacific Northern-type No. 2209 at Denver is a far cry from Ten-wheeler No. 643. (John Aenslic Collection)

One interesting development in passenger service outside the St. Louis Gateway took place when Missouri Pacific took over the Chicago & Eastern Illinois Railroad in 1967. This actually added one passenger train, the *Danville–Chicago Flyer*. This train was basically a long-distance commuter run from Danville to Chicago in the morning, with the return trip in the evening. The train itself was short lived in the MoPac System because the Louisville & Nashville Railroad purchased that portion of the L&N from Woodland Junction to Evansville, Indiana well before Amtrak's creation.

This volume attempts to review MoPac's passenger train services and equipment as they were in the pre-Amtrak years following World War II. A complete history of the Missouri Pacific's passenger train services, reaching back through the "heavyweight" era to the railroad's earliest years, hopefully will be written some day.

The company provided some incredible services during the various periods of economic development in MoPac territory. Although the

Missouri Pacific no longer exists as such within the Union Pacific Railroad system, one can still ride passenger trains over major segments of former MoPac rails as we move into the 21st century.

Missouri Pacific Bus Lines Expands South Texas Service

Missouri Pacific Bus Lines' operations in Texas recently were expanded to provide through service between Houston and Brownsville, Texas, via Corpus Christi.

The new service offers seven daily schedules in each direction between Houston and Corpus Christi and intermediate points; six in each direction between Houston and Brownsville; four in each direction between Alvin and Angleton; four in each direction between Houston, Bay City and Victoria and one in each direction between Bay City and Victoria.

Another service for the convenience of bus patrons living in the Rio Grande Valley recently began with the joint operation of through coaches between Brownsville and other Valley points and San Antonio, Dallas, Fort Worth by the Missouri Pacific Bus Lines and the Greyhound Lines. This new service features a double daily schedule via Corpus Christi and San Antonio.

Depots too tell a story and provide an image for the railroad. The Kirkwood, Missouri, depot, although no longer a stop for *Eagles* and commuter trains, is still served by four Amtrak trains daily. It is a suburban station that clearly could be held up as an example for depot appearances everywhere. Kirkwood is 13.4 miles from St. Louis. (Author)

An unusual operation was the MoPac rail bus service at Baytown, Texas. According to the September 1950 timetable, the company provided rail bus service between Houston and Baytown (just east of Houston on the Gulf Coast). Rail bus No. 605 bore MISSOURI PACIFIC LINES lettering. Note the headlight and pilot. (Bob Lorenz Collection)

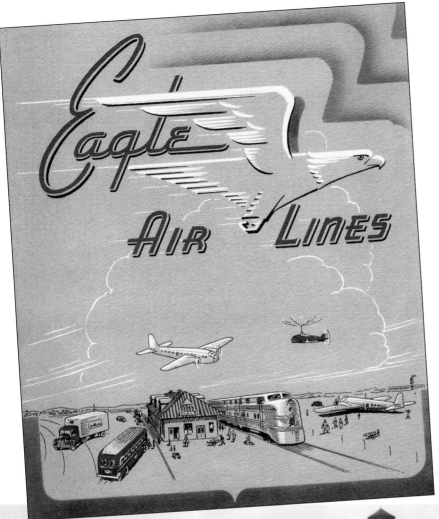

Even as MoPac tried to get into the airline business in the 1940s, streamlined diesel power took over the road's passenger train operations. In the view below, E7 No. 7011 with streamlined equipment, a far cry from the open-end wooden head-end cars and coaches of earlier days. (Airline brochure, Kevin J. Holland Collection; below, Prentice M. Miller, John Aenslic Collection)

USE THE
ST. LOUIS GATEWAY

Traveling to St. Louis? The *Sunshine Special* was the way to go for many decades. It was such a popular train that it was scheduled out of St. Louis in three sections on a daily basis for many years. After World War II, the *Special* was to have been renamed the *Sunshine Eagle* but the company opted for the name *Texas Eagle* instead. Still, the *Texas Eagle* departed St. Louis in two sections, and the *Sunshine Special* continued to operate. In other words, the company continued to dispatch three top trains for Southwestern points every evening, not to mention still other fine trains such as the *Texan*, *Southerner*, and the *Ozarker*. Another set of fine trains operated west to Kansas City, Omaha and Denver; and this list does not include the group operated by the Texas & Pacific.

Although the company was in deep financial trouble, the end of the 1930s marked the begin-

ning of a complete turn around. Changes were made that went virtually unnoticed by the traveling public. For example, the company revised the purchasing and handling of food, supplies, and equipment for the dining cars. In 1939, the company operated 65 dining, dining-lounge, dining parlor, club, grill, and lounge cars. Each car carried approximately $5,000 worth of equipment on the average for food and beverage service. The company was serving approximately 400,000 meals per year. As might be expected, the food service operated at a loss. Except for perhaps the New Haven Railroad, rarely did a railroad turn a profit on its dining cars. Although the company did reduce its dining car expenses by bringing in the purchases and stores department into the buying and storing of food and equipment, it was not enough to produce a profit. However, it was a start in the right direction. The department

became linked with the passenger traffic department, and things improved substantially through centralized buying and storage at the St. Louis coach yards.

The new *Eagle* streamliners were not the only innovation placed in service by the MoPac in 1940. On January 13 of that year, a weekly New York–Mexico City Pullman through-car service went into operation. The car operated via the Pennsylvania Railroad between New York and St. Louis, over the MoPac, Texas & Pacific, and the International-Great Northern (I-GN, a MoPac subsidiary) between St. Louis and Laredo, Texas; and via the National Railways of Mexico (NdeM) between Laredo and Mexico City. The service was operated for the duration of the winter until spring. As might be expected, the through-car service was suspended because of World War II but did resume in 1946.

A westbound MoPac train, heavy with head-end traffic, pulls out of St. Louis Union Station behind E7A No. 7016 on a Spring 1959 morning. Portholes were custom-ordered by MoPac on all of its built-new E-units. (J. Parker Lamb)

Although the *Scenic Limited* was MoPac's fleet leader west, the *Sunshine Special* was the "superb" train service between St. Louis and Texas points. Originating in 1915, the train's popularity grew until finally the company scheduled three *Sunshine Specials* out of St. Louis every night. The trains provided the most up-to-date accommodations of their time. This photo of the *Sunshine Special* was taken in the Arcadia Valley of Missouri around 1920. (Missouri Pacific, Author's Collection)

With the end of the war in 1945, the Missouri Pacific's management could again turn their attention to necessary improvements and innovations in train services. Things moved slowly at first, but one of the first major improvements took place on July 7, 1946. The *Sunshine Special* was extended from St. Louis to New York and Washington, D. C. via the Pennsylvania Railroad. This new train operation included through service between New York City and Mexico City, and was marked by special festivities at the eastern terminals. Ceremonies at Washington Union Station were attended by representatives of the Texas Society of Washington, the Pan American Union, the governments of the United States and Mexico, and the Pennsylvania Railroad.

One of the speakers was Dr. L. S. Rowe, the director of the Pan American Union. He commented that the new rail service marked a milestone in the development of closer relations between the American republics. He added that the new through service to Mexico City was a symbol for the Pan American unity, which in turn would mean so much to the peace and prosperity of the Western hemisphere. Mr. D. C. Young, then a vice president of the Pennsylvania Railroad, commented that his company was proud to be part of such a venture promoting improved international relations.

Ceremonies at Pennsylvania Station in New York City were attended by Enrique Elizondo, the

left: The *Sunshine Special* included an enclosed observation lounge car, as in this 1926 photo at Bismarck, Missouri. (W. F. Thurmond, Author's Collection)

below: The *Scenic Limited* was placed in service by the Missouri Pacific, the Rio Grande, and the Western Pacific railroads in 1915. The MoPac's participation was limited to the operation between St. Louis and Pueblo. The train also handled a Little Rock–Denver Pullman sleeper via Wichita and Geneseo. The *Scenic Limited* was eventually replaced by the *Colorado Eagle* with the same train numbers: 11 and 12. This photo shows train 11 departing St. Louis Union Station prior to 1921. Note the variety of non-air conditioned equipment trailing MoPac's No. 6426. (Missouri Pacific, Author's Collection)

right: This photo of the *Sunshine Special* circa 1925 illustrates the differences and progress of the train during its first ten years of service. Note the differences in motive power, style of equipment and length of train. (Missouri Pacific, Author's Collection)

below: How things changed from 1925–26 to 1948. This photo of a 14-car *Sunshine Special* at Carondelit Park in St. Louis shows one of the final editions of the train. Note the mixture of cars painted in *Eagle* colors as well as Pullman green. (Missouri Pacific, Author's Collection)

Mexican consul general; Mr. J. C. White, a vice president of the PRR; and a wide variety of representatives of the New York City government, the TexasSociety of New York, and the Pan American Union. The program was interspersed with Mexican music provided by a nine-piece orchestra. Senor Elizondo offered congratulations and good wishes from the Mexican government for the new friendships, and expressed hope that the new train service would contribute to the greater mutual knowledge and understanding between the United States and Mexico.

The year 1946 also saw the inauguration of the new *Royal Gorge*, a joint through train operation by the MP and the Rio Grande between St. Louis and Salt Lake City via Pueblo. The *Royal Gorge* made direct connections with the Chicago–Oakland *Exposition Flyer* in both directions at Salt Lake City. In addition, the *Royal Gorge* offered through coach, tourist and first class sleeping car service between St. Louis and Oakland. The train provided additional service on the same route as the *Colorado Eagle*. However, it was a short-lived service and by 1950 only part of the schedules remained in the timetable between Hoisington and Kansas City. It might be remarked that the only portion of the run that was even remotely successful was on the Rio Grande Railroad. The Western Pacific had attempted to operate the *Royal Gorge* through to Oakland, but the business simply was not there and the experiment with the through equipment was very short lived.

Still other 1946 improvements consisted primarily of speeding up schedules and improving turnaround times for passenger equipment in the

top: The *Sunflower* (trains 19 and 20) ran between St. Louis–Kansas City–Omaha, and carried equipment for Trains 419 and 420 between Pleasant Hill and Wichita. Trains 19 and 20 actually operated between St. Louis and Kansas City with 119 continuing to Omaha and 609 to Lincoln. This June 21, 1951, photo shows Train 420 ready to depart Wichita for Pleasant Hill and connection with train 20. (George C. Corey)

middle: Train 120 departs Omaha for Kansas City with Pacific No. 6627 handling nine cars including two Pullmans for St. Louis. The train also offered dining and parlor car service to Kansas City. The westbound counterpart was No. 119. Pullmans on this run were generally 10-1-2 or 12-1s. (A. Robert Johnson)

below: This train at Lincoln, Neb., in late 1950 could be either train 606 or 610 en route from Lincoln to Union. (W. C. Whittaker Collection)

St. Louis terminal. Plans were also being completed for the new *Texas Eagles*, as yet unannounced by the end of 1946.

Between 1946 and 1950, some passenger services were curtailed, mostly in the form of some local trains and various stops being eliminated. The New York City–Mexico City service was completely discontinued by 1948. In its place, the *Aztec Eagle* was established between San Antonio and Mexico City via the MoPac system and the National Railways of Mexico. A "cross-the-platform" service was offered between the *Texas Eagle* and the *Aztec Eagle* at San Antonio.

The through Mexico City sleeper was not re-established until early 1953, when the car was added to the *Texan* between St. Louis and Laredo. During the next few years, the St. Louis–Mexico City sleeper was an "on again, off again" arrangement until the 1960s when the car seemed to be on a permanent basis on the *Texas Eagle/Aztec Eagle*, trains 1 and 2.

As the company rolled into the 1950s, MoPac president Russell L. Dearmont launched a campaign to recapture lost passenger business. The company introduced tray meals and reduced fares substantially on a number of routes. The company had actually decided to abandon or discontinue the *Valley Eagle*, but lower fares brought back the business and the train stayed on.

Lower fares, tray meals, and faster schedules were not the only innovations to be found on the MoPac during the late 1950s. "Thrift-T-Sleeper" was soon a new term in the rail travel dictionary. On June 1, 1958, the company added such a car with a coach fare plus accommodation charge on the *Colorado Eagle* between St. Louis and Denver. Two eight section, three double bedroom, one drawing room cars were taken out of storage and placed into service on the St. Louis–Denver run. Mr. Dearmont reported to *Railway Age* (June 30, 1958, p. 7) that the service was running to capacity and that the car was not taking business away from the rest of the train. Furthermore, he commented, passenger business in the Rio Grande Valley climbed 39 percent within two weeks after the company launched the reduced fares. As 1958

drew to a close, the MoPac was quite pleased with the results of its positive actions and innovative services on both the *Eagles* and the regular passenger train services.

The company was so pleased, in fact, with the Thrift-T-Sleeper service to Colorado, that a new service was added between St. Louis and Hot Springs, Arkansas in January 1959. It could be said that in the late 1950s, the MoPac was one of a few railroads in the United States with any kind of a positive attitude toward rail passenger services.

The company added a new Wichita–Denver sleeper service with the coach ticket-plus-sleeper space charge in May 1959. The new service eliminated the need to change trains in the wee hours of the morning at Geneseo, Kansas, to and from the *Colorado Eagle*. MoPac also applied the same philosophy to the Houston–New Orleans run and Pullman revenues immediately jumped 55%. Still more innovations were on the drawing board.

The last run of Trains 221 and 232 took place on March 22, 1960. By then the train was down to two cars with a steam generator equipped Geep for power. A very good looking train, but hardly profitable. This photo shows train 232 emerging from the 3,136-foot tunnel at Criket, Arkansas. This photo shows the last Train 232 to ever operate on the White River Line. (Wayne Leeman, Missouri Pacific; Author's Collection)

top: Train 821 pauses at El Dorado, Ark., to set out its 8-2-1 Pullman from St. Louis before continuing to Monroe. Train 822 picked up the sleeper for the connection at Gurdon. Southbound this sleeper was handled in the *Sunshine Special*, Train 31 (and No. 1, the *Texas Eagle*). The heavyweight sleeper in this May 1955 view was soon replaced with a 14 roomette, 2 double bedroom, and 1 drawing room car. Trains 821 and 822 were also cut back to a Gurdon–El Dorado operation. (Al Phelps)

middle: A rather heavy Train 15 departs St. Louis for Kansas City on September 5, 1959, behind a single E-unit. Train 15 and its eastbound counterpart, No. 14, were nameless but did provide parlor car service and a dining-lounge car as well as reclining seat coaches. (W. S. Kuba)

bottom: It is October 1961, and Train 15 is as heavy as ever for its run from St. Louis to Kansas City. With one of the classic portholed E7s and two Alco PA's, the train with a heavy consist of head-end cars passes a Frisco switch crew near the Grand Avenue Tower in St. Louis. (W. S. Kuba)

Moving into the 1960s, the MP began offering Slumbercoach service in conjunction with the Baltimore & Ohio between Washington, D.C. and Texas points, and continued to slash fares—even to the point of offering round-trip tickets for the one-way fare plus $1.00. In most cases this worked, but it did virtually nothing for the Kansas City–Newport, Arkansas run, trains 221 and 232. The trains came off. It can be said that although the MoPac had a great deal of faith in the passenger train, it was not simply blind faith.

The MP reported in early 1960 that passenger revenues had increased four percent over 1958 and that passenger train revenues per train-mile had climbed to a ten-year high (*Railway Age*, February 8, 1960, page 7).

The decade of the 1960s could be characterized as one of growth, change, decline, and train-off petitions—all culminating in the debut of Amtrak on May 1, 1971. The last ten years of Missouri Pacific passenger train service were a mixture of just about everything!

With the positive impetus of the late 1950s, the company undertook a massive reconstruction project beginning in late 1961 which lasted until about 1964. The entire passenger car fleet was rebuilt literally from the wheels to the roof. Eight cars per month were rebuilt at the Sedalia, Missouri, shops. Not only were the interiors completely refurbished, but the exteriors were repainted a solid blue with a three-inch band of silver reflective material applied above the window line. Equipment with stainless steel sides and fluted roofs remained unpainted in those areas. The MoPac's herald, white lettering on red, was applied to both sides of the cars. This was a major change from the former blue and gray color scheme in use on the streamlined (and later standard) cars since the *Missouri River Eagle* was introduced in 1940.

Mail and Express Service During the Final Decade Before Amtrak

An incredible service improvement took place in 1963 when the MoPac ordered 50 high-speed, box-express cars from their own De Soto, Missouri, shops. The new 70-foot cars were really a cross between a baggage car and a box car with the placing of the doors, two on each side, and yet the cars were built to freight car specifications. The 50 new cars replaced a like number of 50-foot, double-door box cars that had been converted to box-express cars for passenger service in 1950. The new cars had 34% more floor space, but weighed only 2% more than the cars they replaced. The new cars served in baggage and express service as well as storage mail service on virtually all MoPac passenger trains. They also traveled to Chicago on the Gulf, Mobile & Ohio's mail train out of St. Louis.

The MoPac had also sought other ways to meet needs and speed up the carrying of the U.S. Mail. In mid-1961 piggyback entered the scene, coupled to regular passenger trains. A similar

Alco PA No. 8035 heads up the *Southern Scenic*, Train 221, at Cotter, Arkansas, en route from Kansas City to Newport, Arkansas, via the White River Line. In 1950, the train consist included a through Kansas City–Memphis Pullman and a grill-coach. In this 1955 photo, a single coach handles the markers for the three car train. Note the placement of the words "Missouri Pacific" in the gray band on the Alco PA's. (A. C. Phelps)

MoPac trains navigate
St. Louis Union
Station's complex
trackwork in this pair
of 1950s views. (Both,
H.E. Williams,
TLC Collection)

18

practice was followed by the Great Northern and the Chesapeake & Ohio, but few other roads embraced the intermodal concept in conjunction with their passenger train schedules.

The MoPac, in this case, created a truly innovative operation between St. Louis and Houston. The daily 800-mile coordinated rail-highway mail service permitted one day earlier deliveries to Houston-area residents of mail originating or passing through St. Louis and Texarkana. At the time the operation began, it was the largest and longest piggyback mail service. It eliminated additional handling that had been required with the former all-rail movement and made possible a faster, direct highway delivery of mail to the Houston Post Office each morning.

The system worked liked this: Mail destined for Southwestern cities was loaded directly into two highway trailers already placed on a flat car equipped for passenger service. When loading was complete, the flat car was then switched to the head-end of the MoPac's mail and express special, train No. 37, due to depart St. Louis Union Station at 10:20 p.m.

One of the trailers, carrying Texarkana-area mail, was taken off the train at Texarkana at 11:25 a.m. the next morning. It was replaced by a trailer loaded with Houston mail. A second flat car, with two more Houston-bound trailers, was also added to train 37's consist at Texarkana.

The train was due in at Palestine, Texas, by 8:45 p.m. At that point all four trailers were taken off the train to complete the remainder of the journey (154 miles) to Houston by highway. The trailers were able to reach the Houston post office by 2:00 a.m., early enough to permit sorting the mail for same-day deliveries. This was much faster than the former all-rail routing which required the mail to be unloaded from baggage cars at the Houston depot and loaded into trucks for movement to the post office.

Northbound mail bound for St. Louis and other eastern cities departed Houston at 11:00 p.m., running over the highway to Palestine. The trailers were loaded onto the flat cars for the mail train, which arrived in Texarkana at 11:30 a.m. the next morning, and at St. Louis by 11:00 p.m. In this way, the northbound mail could be delivered to the Texarkana distributing center and to St. Louis without any intermediate handling.

Another interesting facet about this service was that the trailers could be loaded with mail while on the flat car in passenger stations. This eliminated much of the ramping of the trailers and some of the switching of the flat cars.

THE FINAL ROUND

The automobile began to cut even more seriously into the MoPac's passenger business after 1962. Train-off petitions became a way of life from that time on, not only for the Missouri Pacific but all railroad companies. The innovative fares, family plans on a daily basis, tasty tray meals, slumbercoaches, and Thrift-T-Sleepers all seemed to lose out to the Interstate System and what was once a "cheap" gasoline economy. The automobile was definitely perceived to be the least expensive way to travel during the 1960s.

The 1962 timetables still listed a complete set of train services including the *Texas Eagles*, *Aztec Eagle*, *Louisiana Eagle*, *Southerner*, *Westerner*,

top: An April 20, 1963, insurance convention special train is about to depart New Orleans with Pullmans from the MP, Santa Fe and Southern Pacific.

above: Train 8—at Poplar Bluff in 1965— was a nameless run from San Antonio to St. Louis. Services included reclining seat coaches and a grill-coach. Note the piggy-back cars coupled to the rear of the train. (Both, J. W. Swanberg)

19

This Texas & Pacific train is crossing the Huey P. Long Bridge at New Orleans. T&P's overnight train between Houston and New Orleans was known as the *Houstonian*. Daytime services were provided by the *Louisiana Sunshine Special*. Texas & Pacific passenger diesels carried the full MoPac color scheme, but with the T&P insignia on the nose, and the words "Texas & Pacific" in the blue band. (Missouri Pacific, Author's Collection)

Louisiana Daylight, Colorado Eagle, Missourian, Missouri River Eagle, Houstonian, Orleanean, Pioneer, and a set of nameless trains, but yet still offering sleeping cars, grill and dining car services as well as coaches.

During the next two years the list of name trains would decline substantially. The survivors included the *Texas Eagles, Aztec Eagle*, and the *Missouri River Eagle*. There were still four trains each way between St. Louis and Kansas City, but one could see that the situation was becoming more desperate as time went on. Even though the MoPac's financial health was improving, such would not continue if the company was expected to shoulder the increasing financial burden of the passenger train in the environment of the late 1960s. Yet the company continued to operate the trains in a clean and efficient manner.

The time period from 1965 to 1967 was relatively stable. A few short-haul trains continued, such as numbers 37 and 38 between Memphis and Little Rock. However, as 1968 rolled up on the calendar, the company discontinued additional trains between St. Louis and Kansas City, leaving but two trains each way daily. As far as name trains were concerned, only the *Texas Eagles* and *Aztec Eagles* were listed in the September 1, 1968, timetable.

During the next few months into 1969, the company discontinued all sleeping car services. In fact, the last advertisements for sleeping car services were in the Fall 1968 timetable. That was also the last time the Mexico City sleeping car service was in operation. The new 1969 timetables reflected "coach only" services with a dining car between St. Louis and San Antonio. Diner-coaches

operated on the Longview–Fort Worth and Houston–Palestine sections of the *Texas Eagles*; and a grill-coach service remained on the pair of St. Louis–Kansas City trains. The *Texas Eagles* were cut back even further in 1970. Passenger services on the "St. Louis Gateway" in early 1971 were but a whisper of what was offered a decade before, let alone the services offered in the 1940s.

Passenger service on the MoPac routes has been under the jurisdiction of Amtrak since 1971. Services have improved from the dark and bleak year of 1970. After Amtrak, the MoPac continued to operate various types of special passenger trains and owned four business cars and one sleeping car for company service. Ultimately, this equipment was merged into the Union Pacific fleet. However, one can still ride passenger trains over major segments of the MoPac rails in 2003.

This train passing through suburban St. Louis in 1963 appears to be the overnight train from Kansas City, number 18, still known in 1963 as the *Missourian*. The number had been changed from 10 to 18 during the early 1960s. (Bob Lorenz)

MoPac timetables shrank through the 1960s, in step with the trains they advertised. (Author's Collection)

21

THE STREAMLINED EAGLES

The Missouri Pacific Railroad Company ranks among a small number of railroads that operated a streamliner fleet with a common name. There were only a few such lines including the Southern Pacific's *Daylights*, the Milwaukee Road's *Hiawathas*, the Burlington's *Zephyrs*, the Santa Fe *Chiefs*, and the Chicago & North Western's *400s*. All of these were superb trains, and all served different markets—except for the *400s*, *Zephyrs*, and *Hiawathas* competing on the Chicago–Twin Cities route.

The *Eagles* covered a substantial amount of the MP/T&P system. The *Eagles* were not identical by any stretch of the imagination, and were built for specific travel markets. As far as decor and construction were concerned, many of the coaches and sleepers were built to serve in the *Eagle* pool. In that respect, much of the *Eagle* equipment *was* identical, but in terms of train

length and the services offered the trains were quite different.

The first *Eagle* went into service in March 1940 between St. Louis, Kansas City, and Omaha. Known simply as the *Eagle*, the name was changed to the *Missouri River Eagle* when the *Delta Eagle* went into service between Memphis and Talluhah. The *Colorado Eagle* went into operation in 1942, while the *Texas, Louisiana,* and *Valley Eagles* did not grace MP/T&P rails until 1948. The system was also responsible for the *Aztec Eagle* between San Antonio and Laredo, Texas, a through National Railways of Mexico train to and from Mexico City.

The history of the *Eagles* covers the time period from 1940 to 1971. After 1960, passenger patronage declined on these superb trains until 1970 when the entire *Eagle* fleet was but a whisper of its origins. The *Texas Eagle* and St. Louis -

Kansas City trains 14-15 and 16-17 remained until Amtrak Day—May 1, 1971. Nevertheless, the Missouri Pacific continued to operate the trains in a clean and appropriate fashion.

The objective of this chapter is to provide a description of each of the *Eagles,* the types of services offered, dates of operation, and other information concerning the particular trains.

THE MISSOURI RIVER EAGLE

In 1938 business was definitely improving after the long depression which had begun in 1929. Several railroads across the country had placed new streamlined trains in service. Trains such as the Milwaukee Road's *Hiawathas* were bringing the business back to the rails as well as a substantial net income for the passenger accounts for those particular runs. The MoPac was aware of this, and though the railroad was in bankruptcy,

The *Eagles* were not restricted to Missouri Pacific rails. The Denver & Rio Grande Western Railroad handled the *Colorado Eagle*, including motive power, between Pueblo, Colorado, and Denver. In this view, the *Colorado Eagle* is running as D&RGW train No. 4 near Colorado Springs, after its overnight trip from St. Louis.
(Missouri Pacific, Author's Collection)

The *Missouri River Eagle* started the chain of events that led to the entire *Eagle* fleet. The original train consisted of six cars including one baggage, one baggage-mail, two coaches, one food and beverage car, and finally the observation-lounge-parlor car. The *Eagle* operated as trains 5 and 6 between Kansas City and St. Louis and as 105 and 106 between Kansas City and Omaha. The *Eagle* posed for the company camera shortly after its 1940 debut. (J. Michael Gruber Collection)

management knew it would take money to make money. Plans were made to improve the competitive position of the railroad's passenger business, and in 1938, the MP ordered two sets of equipment for a new train service. The equipment consisted of two 2000-hp diesel locomotives, four head-end cars, four coaches, two dining cocktail lounge cars, and two parlor observation cars. The equipment was to be divided into two sets of six cars for each new train, to be called the *Eagle*, and place on an approximately nine-hour schedule between St. Louis and Omaha via Kansas City. The locomotives were ordered from Electro-Motive Corporation (EMC) and the passenger cars were built by American Car & Foundry.

The first complete train was delivered on February 6, 1940, while the second arrived on February 27th. The *Eagle* was then placed on an extensive exhibition tour over the MoPac system prior to going into service on March 10th.

Initially the schedule of the six-car streamliner was as follows: Westbound, the train departed St. Louis at 8:45 a.m. and arrived at Omaha at 5:55 p.m., with a 20 minute stop at Kansas City from 1:45 to 2:05 p.m. Eastbound, the train departed Omaha at 8:40 a.m. and arrived at St. Louis at 5:40 p.m., with a ten-minute stop at Kansas City from 12:30 to 12:40 p.m.

The *Eagles'* AC&F passenger equipment was styled by industrial designer Raymond Loewy. The design of the original streamliner was such that the train appeared as a single-unit streamlined train. This was accomplished by a continuous color scheme from the locomotive to the observation car and by wide winged diaphrams between the cars. The color scheme consisted of a deep blue accented by creamy white lines. A light gray panel was defined by two broad bands of polished aluminum. A unique window treatment was accomplished by varying the rectangular five-foot-

long windows with round portholes which relieved any sense of monotony.

The focal point of the design was the emblem of the train, a stylized eagle, on both the front of the locomotive and on the rear of the observation car. The eagle's widespread, polished metal wings blended with the contours of the engine and gave a considerable amount of emphasis to the motif as a symbol of beauty, strength, and swiftness. The eagle insignia on the rear of the observation car was sculptured in cast aluminum in full relief.

The interior of the equipment was bright, cheery, colorful, and attractive. The treatment of each car was different, but harmonious, so that the passenger had the effect of walking through a tastefully decorated home or apartment of several different rooms.

THE COACHES

The first coach was equipped with 76 seats for local passengers. The second car provided 61 seats for through passengers and offered the ultimate in MoPac coach service at that time. The general features of the coaches were similar. The

This 1940 view of the *Missouri River Eagle* shows the consist to good advantage. Not only did the motive power have the "Eagle-in-Flight" emblem on the nose, but the same was true for the observation parlor car on the rear end. (Missouri Pacific, Author's Collection)

This MoPac publicity photo was one of many taken of the new train prior to its entering service in 1940. Note the porthole windows on E-unit No. 7001, and the style of baggage and RPO-baggage cars on the head end. (Missouri Pacific, Kevin J. Holland Collection)

cars were equipped with deep-pile carpeting, reclining seats, Venetian blinds, and hand loomed curtains. The only difference between the two cars was that in the second or deluxe coach, lounge rooms were also included with the rest rooms.

The color scheme was in varying shades of blue, set off by a pale yellow ceiling. The carpet was a deep rich blue with a soft gray-blue for the walls above the windows and the baggage rack. The chair upholstery was also a deep blue.

The bulkheads were given a surface treatment that contrasted the deep blue satin finish with a silvery tone which was carried through to the passageways. The eagle insignia, designed in red, blue and gray plastic, appeared as an embellishment on the bulkheads. Venetian blinds were of a silver color with hand-loomed curtains, horizontally striped in mulberry and blue against a natural background.

For general car lighting, circular wells of light in the form of specially designed fixtures were set into the ceiling. These gave direct light to the aisles. There were also individually controlled lighting fixtures set into the bottom of the baggage rack that provided direct illumination for reading.

In the deluxe coach, the women's lounge had been screened with blue grass-cloth portiers that appeared against the silver of the passageway. Soft pastels, such as light blue and dusty pink were also combined. The sofa was upholstered in a rose tone. Flooring was pale blue with an off-white inlay. A vanity dressing table was constructed of glass and aluminum. The men's lounge was made up of more masculine materials, such as knotty pine and wood panelling, pigskin upholstery, and flooring of beige with black inlay.

THE DINING-BAR-LOUNGE CAR

The dining-bar-lounge car consisted of four areas. The kitchen was located at one end of the car. The dining room was adjacent to the kitchen and the lounge area was beyond the dining room. The other end of the car, adjacent to the lounge, contained the bar. The dining room could serve 24 passengers at one time, with six tables for four people each. The lounge room was separated from the dining room by a false partition and accommodated 22 passengers. If conditions required, ie., heavy traffic, passengers could have their meals served in the lounge room. The bar area not only served the lounge room, but also served the parlor observation which followed. The make-up of the train required that the bar area be adjacent to the parlor car.

The dining room was separated from the bar-lounge area by a swinging door, on either side of which was a mirror panel etched with fruit, flowers, and vegetable motifs. These mirror panels provided a very distinctive decorative effect.

The ceiling of the car, which was of silver opalescent lacquer, was curved into the bulkheads to give a flowing continuity to the interior architectural and decorative design. The soft sheen of silver was repeated in the aluminum Venetian blinds that were used for the wide windows. Above the windows was a light trough accented with strips of translucent plastic that ran the entire length of the section. Flourescent lights were set into this trough which was designed to reflect the light downward on the tables and upward on the walls above the windows. On this wall section, a new decorative fabric with a rose and silver opaline surface was used, and the upward rays of the flourescent light highlighted the beauty and reflecting quality of luminous material. Ceiling wells of fluorescent light, shaded with large plastic sheets, were used for the general illumination of the dining room.

The general color scheme of the dining car was built around harmonous contrasts, such as gray-blue used for the side ceiling and silver rose for the drapery. These tones were strengthened by the deeper tone of the rose-taupe upholstery, dramatic emphasis being given by the rich claret-red of the carpeting.

The bar and lounge sections were divided by glass panels and achieved a club-like atmosphere with its four intimate bridge groupings in the lounge area, and the bar section with its friendly built-in seats. Windows in the lounge section were grouped to make one large unit. An aluminum frame outlined the window group with hand-loomed rough-texture curtains of blue fabric at either end. Lighting fixtures that gave pleasent, glareless illumination were set into the lowered side ceiling to throw direct light rays on the bridge tables. Glass fixtures reflecting their light against the spun aluminum inverted bowls provided additional lighting. Decorative wood pier panels, carved and sandblasted in oak, portrayed two figures symbolizing American agriculture and industry.

At the far end of the car, a curved bar predominated. The bar was most attractive and included a facing of bright blue. Set into the blue background were 14 lighted circles which depicted the flowers of the states the MoPac served. There was a large color mural painted on aluminum on the back wall of the bar which symbolized the speed and swiftness of the streamliner as well as its emblem, the eagle.

Another early publicity view of the new *Eagle*, airbrushed to accent the cars' clean lines. (Missouri Pacific, Kevin J. Holland Collection)

The *Missouri River Eagle* in September 1948, behind F-units. The eastbound *Eagle*, train 106, is about to depart Omaha for Kansas City and St. Louis. (Elmer Treloar, Author's Collection)

In the bar-lounge section, the soft gray tones of the heavy pile carpet acted as a foil for the yellow leather upholstery and the blue walls and draperies. Deep yellow on the side ceiling picked up the upholstery color. The table tops were made of pearl gray Formica to contrast with the burgundy built in seats adjoining the bar. The bulk-head was decorated with silver and opalescent which contrasted pleasantly with the mirrors at the other end of the room.

The ceiling of the bar area was lower than the lounge section, for a more intimate feeling. It was painted blue, a very effective combination with the walnut of the walls. There were two built-in

sofas upholstered in burgundy needlepoint. Individual lights over these seats provided lighting for passengers. The window arrangement above the sofas comprised more porthole windows.

THE PARLOR OBSERVATION CAR

The last car of this beautiful train accommodated 36 passengers in all. The parlor section contained 26 revenue seats, while the drawing room accommodated five more passengers. The observation end provided seating for five people. The car provided luxurious comfort in an atmosphere of quiet dignity. The parlor seats were swivel lounge chairs with reclining backs. The upholstery fabric colors were baxter brown and sea green. The windows were grouped into large areas and the window sills were widened to form a shelf for snacks, magazines, etc. The baggage racks were built in and extended the entire length of the parlor section. There were individually controlled lights over each seat, which were soft and glareless.

The observation room contained a built-in radio, two fixed sofas and four deep-seated lounge chairs. A clock and speedometer, designed in aluminum and plastic, decorated the wall.

The drawing room had all the comforts and appointments of a private club room, with comfortable built-in sofa, moveable chairs, built-in cabinets and table lamps. One of the walls was panelled in old Claro Walnut Marlight as a contrast to the apple green of the other three walls. For the window treatment, a deep aluminum reveal was used to house the Venetian blinds and draperies. Built-in lights above the sofa provided direct lighting for reading and illuminated the Currier & Ives prints of old locomotives that were framed for all decorations.

The interior color scheme of the parlor car was most relaxing. The car was done with a pale yellow ceiling and walls while the baggage racks were apple green with a dado of deep sea green. Venetian blinds were rose-beige with the draperies a matching rose-beige pattern fabric. The carpet was of rose-mahogany and added a strengthening note to the color scheme which carried through to the observation end. There the carpet tone was repeated in the dado and offered a contrast to the various shades of blue-greens that were used for the Venetian blinds, upholstery and drapery fabrics.

CONSTRUCTION

The six cars of each original *Eagle* shared the same type of body shell, and were designed to fully meet the requirements of the United States Railroad Post Office specifications and also the American Association of Railroad (AAR) specifications for new passenger equipment.

Both ends of all cars were equipped with wide winged diaphrams which included vestibule curtains and tailgates on the passenger-carrying cars. The trap doors in the vestibules were made of aluminum and operated in conjunction with the folding steps, which in turn formed a continuous line with side skirts when closed.

This rear view of Train 106 departing Omaha reveals a rebuilt standard coach as the third car on September 17, 1948. For a short distance, the *Eagle* will operate over the Union Pacific before running on MoPac rails to Kansas City. (Elmer Treloar, Author's Collection)

The new *Eagles'* brake equipment was the latest design of that time, providing electro-pneumatic operation with the addition of speed governor valves on the baggage-mail and observation parlor cars. National tight-lock couplers were utilized, as well as rubber-type draft gears, to minimized slack action and its attendant discomfort.

Four-wheel trucks were used on all of the cars. The trucks were equipped with sound-deadening materials at the bolster springs, and body side bearings to completely isolate the truck noises from the car body.

Train 16, the Missouri River Eagle, arriving at Jefferson City, Mo., on May 28, 1965. (Howard S. Patrick)

Train 17 is shown here near Eureka on May 6, 1967. A far cry from the original consist, this head-end heavy *Eagle* has 11 cars with a coach and grill-coach bringing up the rear. (William S. Kuba)

The passenger carrying cars were air-conditioned, and all cars included steam heat during the winter months. The kitchen of the dining bar lounge car was outfitted with stainless steel equipment, which included cooking ranges, refrigerators, sinks and electric dishwasher.

The equipment for these first *Eagles* was most pleasant to ride, and succeeded in one of its primary objectives—luring passengers back to MoPac rails.

OPERATIONS

From March 10, 1940, through September 30th of that year, the new *Eagle* got off to a roaring start. During those first six and a half months of operation, the train was on time 96.3% of the time at both terminals. The new *Eagle* carried a total of 81,156 passengers for 1,868,400 passenger-miles. The average number of passengers per trip was 198, and the *Eagle* was earning $1.81 per mile. The overall scheduled speed for the original schedule was slightly over 53 miles per hour. The management was pleased back in St. Louis.

From September 1940 to September 1941 things were even better. The *Eagle* carried 162,156 passengers for an average of 222 passengers per trip. Revenue was up to $1.92 per train-mile. However, as positive as things were prior to the

Second World War, the MoPac was not content to let things just happen.

The train served very important cities along the route from St. Louis to Omaha via Kansas City. However, the *Eagle* missed the capital of Nebraska, which was just 47.7 miles from the MoPac's main line at Union, a junction for a branch line to Lincoln. The railroad decided to tap the business potential of Lincoln by placing in service a streamlined self-propelled motor car, which made direct connections with the *Eagle* in both directions at Union. The MoPac placed an order with American Car & Foundry in early 1941 for the new car to be delivered in the fall of that year.

The connecting train to Lincoln was a very neat, streamlined, double-ended "Motorailer" that was capable of speeds of up to 70 miles per hour. The Union–Lincoln service was very convenient, with the railroad operating the car two round trips per day. The train connected with each of the *Eagles* in both directions. The car was maintained at the Lincoln enginehouse.

The Motorailer was arranged with a center vestibule, a baggage compartment at one end to carry 10,000 pounds, and a passenger compartment at the end seating 34. The interior finish and trim in the coach section and the exterior color scheme matched the mainline *Eagle* trains. In addition, the coach section was air-conditioned.

Power was supplied by two Waukesha 210-horsepower underbody-mounted spark-ignition oil engines. Twin Disc clutches and torque converters transmitted power to geared driven axles, each engine driving one truck. The engines were capable of accelerating the car to its top speed of 70 miles per hour in 3-1/2 minutes, over a distance of 2.6 miles on level tangent track.

The center vestibule was built with open step wells. The lower step revolved through 90 degrees and carried a section of skirt so that in the closed position of the step the skirt line was continuous. The coach section was equipped with reclining seats of the revolving type as the car was not turned at the ends of the runs.

The passenger compartment was lit by safety center ceiling fixtures which had blue night lights built in, and by individual lights in the safety basket racks over each seat. The floor was covered with carpeting. There were Venetian blinds on the windows, and also drapes between the windows.

The side sashes in the passenger compartment were double glazed, with the inner glass being shatterproof. The sash at the ends of the car had single-glazed, shatterproof glass.

The operator's cabs at each end of the car were completely enclosed, with the upper partitions of the side, rear, and door of the cab made of glass.

The car could have been called a "Mini-Eagle" as it was a very luxurious piece of equipment for the assignment. It matched the mainline *Eagle* in almost every way, and the car was extremely dependable. On those days that it was in the shops, a modernized 4-4-2 steam locomotive would handle a combination coach-baggage car between Union and Lincoln.

The Motorailer ran nearly 200 miles each day during its two round trips. Because of the service provided by the unique streamliner motor car, the MoPac was successful in securing business from the Nebraska state capital that it otherwise would not have obtained. The car, initially, did a very good job for the Missouri Pacific.

An interesting aspect of the Union–Lincoln run was that during its two round trips to connect with the eastbound and westbound *Eagles*, the motor car also made simultaneous connections with the MP's overnight St. Louis–Omaha train.

This train service was discontinued between Union and Lincoln in the mid-1950s and replaced by a bus. The bus also made two round

There was more to the *Missouri River Eagle* than simply the St. Louis–Omaha services. The Union to Lincoln, Nebraska, connecting train for the *Eagle* was handled by this self-propelled rail car. Truly a pocket streamliner in its own right, car 670 provided the consist for trains 605 and 606 on a daily basis between the two points. Painted in the *Eagle* color scheme, the ACF car was highly appropriate operating as the *Missouri River Eagle* connection. After the connecting Union–Lincoln rail service was replaced by a bus, car 670 was assigned to other branchline local services, including the remains of the *Delta Eagle* for a short time. (Missouri Pacific, Author's Collection)

trips daily providing connecting service to and from Lincoln for the *Eagle* and the overnight train. The "mini-streamliner's" career was over, but it had left a mark in the history of the *Eagles*.

THE DELTA EAGLE

The *Delta Eagle* began service on May 11, 1941, as a two-car streamliner between Memphis, Tennessee, and Tallulah, Louisiana, a distance of 259 miles. This particular train served an area along the west bank of the Mississippi River that was not only without streamliner service, but without any kind of through public transportation, either rail or bus.

The *Delta Eagle* served a rather interesting territory from a transportation geography standpoint. Between Memphis and Helena, a distance of 76 miles, the land was primarily in cotton production. The area was thickly populated with more than enough paved roads for that period of time. The principal communities are Marianna

and Helena, which during that time were supported by the hardwood lumber industry.

South of Helena, the population became less dense until the area of Snow Lake. There, the route of the *Eagle* traveled through the delta country of the White and Arkansas Rivers, a swampy and nearly inaccessible region with few inhabitants. McGehee is 39 miles south of Snow Lake and 91 miles from Tallulah, the southern terminal of the *Delta Eagle* deep into Louisiana. McGehee, by the way, was a junction of the MoPac's Lake Providence, Monroe, and Wynne Subdivisions of the Louisiana Division and is still an important point for MoPac successor Union Pacific.

In addition to the train services provided by the *Eagle* to Memphis in the morning, and from Memphis in the evening, the MoPac provided a bus connection to and from Greenville. The train stopped at Lake Village for the bus connection.

Prior to the new *Eagle* going into service, the MP operated six demonstration trips into

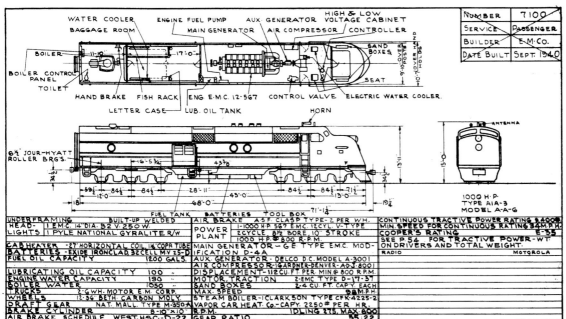

WATER COOLER · ENGINE FUEL PUMP · AUX. GENERATOR · HIGH & LOW VOLTAGE CABINET
BAGGAGE ROOM · MAIN GENERATOR · AIR COMPRESSOR · CONTROLLER
BOILER · SAND BOXES
BOILER CONTROL PANEL · TOILET · SEAT
HAND BRAKE · FISH RACK · ENG. E.M.C. 12-567 · CONTROL VALVE · ELECTRIC WATER COOLER.
LETTER CASE · LUB. OIL TANK · HORN
6½" JOUR-HYATT ROLLER BRG'S.
ANTENNA
1000 H.P. TYPE AIA-3 MODEL A-A-G

NUMBER	7100
SERVICE	PASSENGER
BUILDER	E.M.CO.
DATE BUILT	SEPT. 1940

UNDERFRAMING BUILT-UP WELDED	AIR BRAKE A.S.F. CLASP TYPE - 2 PER WH.	CONTINUOUS TRACTIVE POWER RATING 16000#
HEAD-LIGHTS 1 EMC 14"DIA. 32 V. 250 W.	POWER PLANT 1-1000 H.P. 567 EMC. 12CYL. V-TYPE / 2 CYCLE 8½ BORE 10" STROKE / 1000 H.P. @ 800 R.P.M.	MIN. SPEED FOR CONTINUOUS RATING 34 M.P.H.
CAB HEATER .27 HORIZONTAL COIL 1" COPR TUBE	MAIN GENERATOR - GE TYPE EMC. MODIFICATION D-4A	COOPER'S RATING E-55
BATTERIES -EXIDE IRONCLAD 32 CELL MV 25-D		SEE P. 54 FOR TRACTIVE POWER-WT ON DRIVERS AND TOTAL WEIGHT.
FUEL OIL CAPACITY 1200 GALS.	AUX. GENERATOR - DELCO D.C. MODEL A-3001	RADIO MOTOROLA
LUBRICATING OIL CAPACITY 100	AIR COMPRESSOR -GARDNER-DENVER-AD.J.8001	
ENGINE WATER CAPACITY 190	DISPLACEMENT-112 CU.FT. PER MIN @ 800 R.P.M.	
BOILER WATER 1050	MOTOR, TRACTION 2-EMC TYPE D-17-37	
TRUCKS 2-GWH. MOTOR E.M. CORP.	SAND BOXES 2-4 CU.FT. CAPY EACH	
WHEELS 12-36" BETH. CARBON MOLY.	MAX. SPEED 98 M.P.H.	
DRAFT GEAR NAT. MALL. TYPE M-350-A	STEAM BOILER -CLARKSON TYPE CFK-4225-2	
BRAKE CYLINDER 8-10"X10"	VAPOR CAR HEAT. Co.-CAPY. 2250# PER HR.	
AIR BRAKE SCHEDULE WEST. HSC-D-22	R.P.M. IDLING 275, MAX. 800	
	GEAR RATIO 55:22	

MoPac No. 7100 was custom built by Electro-Motive, with a baggage compartment in the space normally occupied by an E-unit's second diesel powerplant. (Electro-Motive, Kevin J. Holland Collection)

This MoPac diagram shows how the unit's interior was laid out. (Author's Collection)

Memphis carrying goodwill tourists from towns along the train's route. The new *Eagle* was also placed on display for five days. In most of the towns and villages, the entire population turned out to see the new streamliner.

Through some advance thinking and planning for the thinly populated area, the schedule of the train was arranged to suit the convenience of the local towns as much as possible, and also with some regard for connections with other MP trains. The original schedule provided that the northbound *Delta Eagle* would arrive in Memphis at 12:35 p.m. Southbound, the train departed at 4:30 p.m. with a 10:55 p.m. arrival in Tallulah.

The *Delta Eagle* was also conveniently tied into through schedules. On the northbound run, the MP train from New Orleans, Alexandria, and Monroe made close connections for *Eagle* passengers for Pine Bluff, Little Rock, and other points. On the southbound run, in addition to the connections at Memphis, the *Eagle* exchanged passengers with a southbound train from Little Rock to New Orleans at McGehee.

The train itself was very comfortable. It was powered by a 1000-hp diesel-electric locomotive built by Electro-Motive. It was delivered in September 1940 and used in regular service between Memphis and Wynne until the new *Eagle* service was established. In addition to the power unit, the body contained a 19-1/2 foot baggage section. The locomotive was so designed that it could have been easily converted to 2000-hp if required.

The two air-conditioned coaches were designed specifically for this particular train. Built by St. Louis Car, the carbodies were built of low-carbon, high-tensile steel and the decorative design was similar to that of the *Missouri River Eagle* described earlier.

The cars were 78 feet long. The first car contained a 15-foot Railway Post Office section and had a coach capacity of 60 passengers with rest rooms for men and women. The rear coach contained seats for 48 passengers, along with two attractive and commodious lounge and rest rooms.

A lunch counter grill was situated in the forward section of the second car. Two tables seating four each, and three stools at the counter, were available for passengers as well as tray service to individual seats. Although the kitchen area was quite small, it was designed so that anything from sandwiches to steak dinners could be served.

The *Delta Eagle* was one of the shortest-lived *Eagles* on the Missouri Pacific. Launched in 1941, the train as an *Eagle* was discontinued in 1952. In its place, a pair of local trains, Nos. 334 and 335, operated between Helena and McGehee. No. 335 arrived at McGehee in time to connect with the northbound *Sunshine Special* (en route from New Orleans to St. Louis) to provide overnight service from the Delta country to St. Louis. Trains 334 and 335 were discontinued in 1960 and rail passenger service was no more for the Delta country of the White and Arkansas Rivers.

An interesting bit of trivia is that the Missouri Pacific had originally decided to name the train the *Dixie Eagle*. However, it was later decided to name the train the *Delta Eagle* because of the type of geography through which the train traveled.

The *Delta Eagle* goes down in history as being one of those innovations designed for thinly populated regions. The train was moderately successful, especially through the Second World War. However, patronage sagged from the mid-1940s and there was no other choice than to discontinue the train. It probably could be said that the *Eagle* would not have lasted as long as it did had it not been for the war. The important thing about the *Delta Eagle* is that it illustrated the type of thinking that was going on within MP management ranks as they began to pull the company up by its bootstraps. Remember, the MoPac was in bankruptcy and the train was going into operation on the heels of the Great Depression. The design and

type of service offered by the *Delta Eagle* was a tribute to MoPac's train service innovations.

THE COLORADO EAGLE

The third streamlined *Eagle*, the *Colorado Eagle*, entered service on June 21, 1942, serving the St. Louis–Denver market, a distance of 1,015 miles. For the third year in a row, the MoPac had added a new streamliner. However, 1942 was a war year, and the company had been specifically instructed not to make even the slightest announcement of the new train. This was during a period of time when all of the available space for

military personnel was needed, and travel by the general public was discouraged.

The history of the *Colorado Eagle* goes back to early 1941 when the Federal District Court (remember the MoPac's bankruptcy) authorized the company to purchase two diesel-powered streamliners for operation between Denver and St. Louis. Shortly thereafter, the company placed an order with Electro-Motive for four 2000-hp passenger E-units. The company also ordered two diner-lounge cars, four deluxe coaches, two mail cars, two mail-baggage cars, and a mail storage car from the Budd Company.

Four sleeping cars were also to be assigned to the new *Eagle* by the Pullman Company, and were part of a group already under construction for operation on Chicago & North Western, Union Pacific, and Southern Pacific trains. The four cars were of the 6-section, 6-roomette and 4-double bedroom (6-6-4) variety and carried the names *Arkansas River*, *Eagle River*, *Gunnison River*, and *Colorado River*.

The new trains operated via the MP between St. Louis and Pueblo, Colorado, and over the D&RGW beyond to Denver. The original consist included a two-unit locomotive, one mail car, one

The *Colorado Eagle* provided overnight service between St. Louis and Denver. Train 11 westbound and 12 eastbound, it operated over MoPac to and from Pueblo, and via the Rio Grande Railroad beyond. MoPac was an early operator of dome cars. They debuted on the *Colorado Eagle* in 1948. (Missouri Pacific, Kevin J. Holland Collection)

mail-baggage, two coaches, one diner-lounge, and two Pullman sleeping cars. It was one of very few new trains entering service during the war.

The new train ran with capcity crowds continuously through the war. As 1945 rolled around, plans were being quietly made by the MP not only for new trains, but also for improvements in the *Colorado Eagle*.

In 1948, the train received new dome coaches from the Budd Company. A year later, four 10 roomette, 6 double bedroom cars were constructed by Budd for the St. Louis–Denver *Eagle* domeliner.

These were not the only changes made for the *Colorado Eagle* to meet travelers' needs. A new through St. Louis–Los Angeles Pullman sleeper

Another heavily airbrushed MoPac publicity view, this time of the brand-new *Colorado Eagle*. (Missouri Pacific, TLC Collection)

A pair of portholed E-units leads the *Colorado Eagle* at Jefferson City, Mo., in 1944. (TLC Collection)

was added to train 11 between St. Louis and Kansas City, where the car was switched into the consist of the Rock Island's *Golden State*. Returning, the L.A.–St. Louis Pullman was handled by MoPac's train 20, the *Sunflower*. The St. Louis–L.A. through Pullman service continued until the 1950s.

Still another equipment change was the utilization of 10-6 and 14-4 sleepers between St. Louis and Denver instead of the 6-6-4 originally purchased for the trains. The company also added a standard heavyweight sleeper containing 8 sections, 1 drawing room, and 3 double bedrooms between Wichita and Denver in both directions. The 8-1-3 sleepers were handled by trains 411 and 412 between Wichita and Geneseo, at which point the Pullmans were switched in or out of Nos. 11 and 12, respectively.

Besides the dome coach previously mentioned, the *Colorado Eagle* also carried a grill-coach to supplement its diner-lounge car. As the *Colorado Eagle* approached 1952—its tenth year of service—trains 11 and 12 were bigger and better than ever.

The summertime consists of Nos. 11 and 12 for the overnight St. Louis–Denver run were always longer than the fall and spring consists. Usually this meant extra Pullmans and coaches, but regular sleeping cars were also added.

The company added an innovation known as the Thrift-T-Sleeper to the *Colorado Eagle* during the late 1950s. This was an 8-1-3 Pullman between St. Louis and Denver offering accommodations at the coach fare plus a small fee for a berth or bedroom.

As the *Colorado Eagle* approached its 20th year of service, the MP was operating first-class Pullman services (a 10-6 sleeper) between St. Louis and Denver, and a 6-6-4 Pullman between Wichita and Denver. Two Thrift-T-Sleepers (an 8-1-3 and a 6-6-4) operated between St. Louis and Denver as well as coaches, the dome coach, the grill-coach, and the diner lounge. A parlor car was also part of the consist between St. Louis and Kansas City in both directions. However, after

The E-units originally assigned to the *Colorado Eagle* bore customized nose emblems advertising the train's name and its two operators. (Missouri Pacific, Kevin J. Holland Collection)

The *Colorado Eagle* passes Eureka, Missouri, in June 1951. The 11-car train is perfectly matched from the locomotive to the last car. (George C. Corey)

Even though the E-units originally assigned to the *Colorado Eagle* bore joint Missouri Pacific-Rio Grande lettering under their customized eagle nose decorations, they were also assigned to other trains, especially in later years. No. 7003 led the southbound *Texas Eagle* at San Antonio, Texas, in September 1950. (Harold K. Vollrath Collection)

1962, it became more and more obvious that the *Colorado Eagle* was beginning to suffer from the broader decline in passenger traffic. Pullman car services were being dropped one by one. The Wichita Pullman was gone by 1962. The grill-coach and the St. Louis–Kansas City parlor car were also dropped during the early 1960s.

The *Colorado Eagle* lost its name by 1965 and was simply listed in the timetables as trains 11 and 12. Sleeping car services were gone, but the train did carry a diner-parlor between St. Louis and Kansas City. It was "coach only" between Kansas City and Denver. In 1966, trains 11 and 12 made their last runs and a grand train was given up. The *Colorado Eagle* never saw its 25th birthday.

continued on page 45

With its perfectly matched gray-and-blue cars, the *Colorado Eagle* was a sight to behold, particularly after the 1948 introduction of domes. (Both, TLC Collection)

above: Train No. 3, the *Colorado Eagle*, passes Castle Rock, Colorado, on December 13, 1942.

middle: MoPac E3 No. 7000 leads a heavy-weight *Royal Gorge* over D&RGW rails at Eads, Colorado, on February 5, 1950.

bottom: On July 4, 1956, MoPac E8A No. 7018 leads the *Colorado Eagle* out of Denver. (All, Otto Perry/Denver Public Library Western History Collection)

40

above: The *Colorado Eagle*, near Acequia, Colorado, in 1958. (Otto Perry/Denver Public Library Western History Collection)

middle: The *Colorado Eagle* paused at Colorado Springs on July 11, 1960. (Richard J. Wilhelm, Author's Collection)

below: PA-2 No. 8017 led Train 3 near Larkspur, Colorado, in the early 1960s. (Otto Perry/Denver Public Library Western History Collection)

top: This 1959 photo shows No. 11 passing Grand Avenue Tower in St. Louis, bound for Kansas City and Denver.

middle: By 1962, a new blue paint scheme was being applied to motive power and passenger equipment. Motive power was being renumbered from the 7000s and 8000s to less than 100. Alco PA No. 71 led the *Colorado Eagle* at Palmer Lake, Colorado. The trains were no longer perfectly matched. (Both, William S. Kuba)

below: This 1948 view of the *Colorado Eagle* shows a consist of ten cars—including two new Budd domes—near Kirkwood, Missouri. Normally, the *Colorado Eagle* handled two or three head-end cars, one dome coach, one or two regular coaches, one grill-coach, one dining lounge, and a variety of Pullmans. (Missouri Pacific, Author's Collection)

above: Reflecting a transition in MoPac paint schemes, the *Colorado Eagle* leaves Denver in the 1960s

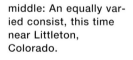

middle: An equally varied consist, this time near Littleton, Colorado.

bottom: Even though MoPac management simplified its passenger paint scheme with the adoption of solid blue, the stainless steel nose eagles brought back memories of the *Eagles'* grander days. (All, Otto Perry/Denver Public Library Western History Collection)

top: E8A No. 40 led a short Colorado Eagle out of Denver. (Otto Perry/Denver Public Library Western History Collection)

middle: The *Colorado Eagle* on the D&RGW at South Denver on June 23, 1963. The domeliner required three passenger units for power on its overnight run between St. Louis and Denver. (Lou Schmitz Collection)

below: By 1963, head-end traffic was a little heavier and the *Colorado Eagle* still merited three units for motive power. This photo shows the train at Palmer Lake en route to Denver. Note the full REA Express car on the head end. (William S. Kuba)

THE TEXAS EAGLES

The planning for the superb *Texas Eagles* began during the early 1940s. In fact, the MP ordered 72 cars with the same interiors and exterior decor as described earlier in this chapter for the *Missouri River Eagle* and *Colorado Eagle*. The equipment included combination and mail cars, coaches, diners, dining-lounge cars, coach-dormitory cars, and Pullman sleeping cars. This equipment was purchased for service on all of the *Eagles* and not simply for the *Texas Eagles*, of which there would be two such trains to southern and western Texas.

Originally the MoPac had decided to call the new Texas trains the *Sunshine Eagles*. By 1947, however, the name was changed to the *Texas Eagles* with the two-section operation. Actually, the two *Texas Eagles* took over two of the three sections of the conventional train, the *Sunshine Special*. The *Sunshine Special* continued to operate with one train after the pair of *Texas Eagles* went into service on August 15, 1948.

The *West Texas Eagle* served the St. Louis–Fort Worth–El Paso market with a through operation over the Texas & Pacific while the *South Texas Eagle* operated between St. Louis and San Antonio. Other cities served included Galveston and Houston, plus a Memphis connection to and from Little Rock.

Dome coaches were added to the *Texas Eagles* in 1952, and new sleepers were placed in operation in 1956. This equipment would be the only new cars added to the Texas trains during the period 1948 to 1971, along with a pair of Slumbercoaches leased in 1959 for service on the *Texas Eagles*. One was leased from the Baltimore & Ohio, while the other came direct from the Budd Company. Through a joint arrangement, the B&O and MoPac offered through Slumbercoach service between Baltimore and Texas. The Missouri Pacific operated the equipment between St. Louis and San Antonio and experienced a 71% average occupancy. MoPac's Slumbercoach service was quietly ended before 1965 and the cars were returned to their owners.

A variety of meal innovations, coach fares in Pullmans, and schedule adjustments could not compensate for the decrease in passenger patronage. From 1964 through 1970, the MoPac system trimmed the *Texas Eagles* from serving El Paso, Memphis, Palestine, and Houston; eventually Fort Worth and San Antonio lost the *Eagles*. By 1970, the *Texas Eagle* simply operated between St. Louis and Texarkana.

There were few trains in North America at that time scheduled as two-section operations. The *Texas Eagles* were combined into one section

The long *Texas Eagles* looked equally good behind either Electro-Motive Division E-units with their distinctive porthole windows, or what is now considered to be a classic among locomotive designs, the Alco PA. With steam lifting the safety valves, Alco PA No. 8014 pauses with Train 1 at the Poplar Bluff depot. Trains 1 and 21 were scheduled into Poplar Bluff only minutes apart. Train 1 was allowed 20 minutes for servicing while 21 was granted a quarter of an hour. This photo was taken by the MoPac photographer in 1952. (Missouri Pacific, Author's Collection)

above: The *Texas Eagles* were a fleet in their own right. With two trains daily in each direction to and from the St. Louis gateway, other sections of the *Texas Eagles* served East and West Texas and points such as Lake Charles and Memphis. This consist posed in Carondelet Park in St. Louis in 1948, southbound on the Arkansas Division. (Missouri Pacific, Author's Collection)

right: It is just after New Year's Day in 1965 as northbound No. 2, the *Texas Eagle*, approaches Austin, Texas, with an eight-car consist. (J. Parker Lamb)

The TEXAS EAGLES
A New Name in Southwestern Travel

Four new, Diesel-powered streamliners, to be called The Texas Eagles, soon will be placed in service by the Missouri Pacific Lines. They will operate on fast, through daily schedules between St. Louis and the principal cities of Texas. Swift, smooth-riding, luxuriously beautiful and comfortable, the new Eagles will be well-prepared to maintain the Missouri Pacific's traditions of travel leadership throughout the Southwest.

around 1962, and even at that, it was an enormously long train. There were still eight sleepers in and out of St. Louis alone, not to mention six coaches and two dining-lounge cars.

Missouri Pacific was most optimistic about the *Eagle* passenger services, but the sad economic facts forced the discontinuances mentioned earlier. Although the *Texas Eagle* was discontinued on May 1, 1971, one can still ride the route of the *Eagle* between St. Louis and San Antonio on Amtrak (see Chapter 6).

continued on page 50

The *Texas Eagles* were combined between St. Louis and Texarkana in 1961. At Texarkana, train 1 was split into the Houston–San Antonio and the El Paso sections. Train 1 operated as the El Paso section, while train 21 continued to Palestine, where it in turn was split into the Houston and San Antonio sections. The Houston section operated as train 121. Train consists in excess of twenty cars into and out of St. Louis were quite common during the early 1960s. In this August 1966 view at St. Louis Union Station, No. 1 is departing for the west. (J. W. Swanberg)

right: The San Antonio section of the *Texas Eagle* in this 1965 view has a seven-car consist including a B&O 16 duplex roomette, 4 double bedroom sleeper behind the RPO-baggage. The normal sleeping car assignment for the San Antonio section included one car each for San Antonio and Mexico City.

below: Train No. 2 heads into Austin in 1964 as a southbound freight waits in the clear. A switch crew with a Geep waits for both trains to clear. (Both, J. Parker Lamb)

The southbound San Antonio
section of the *Texas Eagle* was
photographed approaching
Austin in 1964. The train carries
cars for No. 1, the *Aztec Eagle*,
which operated between San
Antonio, Laredo, and Mexico City.
(J. Parker Lamb)

The *Valley Eagle* provided a daytime run between Houston and Brownsville. Trains 11 and 12 carried a through St. Louis–Corpus Christi coach to and from Houston for connection with the *Texas Eagle*. As train 11 set out the Corpus Christi coach, it also picked up a San Antonio–Brownsville coach from Train 205, the San Antonio–Corpus Christi service. (Missouri Pacific, Author's Collection)

E7A No. 7005 led the *Louisiana Eagle* at Baton Rouge, La., in June 1961. (Harold K. Vollrath Collection)

THE VALLEY EAGLE

The *Valley Eagle* was an all-coach streamliner that went into daylight service between Houston and Brownsville, Texas, on October 31, 1948. The train consisted of coaches and a grill-coach for meals and refreshments. The *Valley Eagle* was the daytime counterpart of the overnight *Pioneer* on the same route.

The *Valley Eagle* was a relatively stable train without much change in the daytime schedule over its nearly 14 years of operation. In an effort to stimulate business, MoPac slashed fares nearly 50% in 1958. This was reasonably successful over the short run, but by 1961 business on the *Valley Eagle* had fallen off to the point that the MoPac decided to apply for the train's discontinuance. The train was finally discontinued during first half of 1962. The July 1962 timetable change made no mention of the *Valley Eagle*.

When the Missouri Pacific was planning the *Valley Eagle*, it was also planning a companion train on the same route to be known as the *Nueces Eagle*. The writer was unable to determine if the

names of the trains were to be two separate sets of trains, ie., a double-daily run in each direction; or if the train was to be named the *Valley* in one direction and the *Nueces* in the other. Regardless, the *Nueces Eagle* never went into service.

THE LOUISIANA EAGLE

The *Louisana Eagle* was a Texas & Pacific Railroad overnight coach-Pullman streamliner between New Orleans and Fort Worth. The overnight train operated on a relatively stable schedule for the 552-mile run from October 10, 1948, through 1962, when the train was combined with the *Texas Eagle* between Marshall and Fort Worth.

The *Louisiana Eagle* drew equipment from the *Eagle* passenger equipment pool and always included a dining-lounge car for meal and beverage service. The *Louisiana Eagle* was discontinued in 1970, about one year before Amtrak's debut.

THE AZTEC EAGLE

Still another *Eagle* that operated on the MoPac was the not-so-well-known *Aztec Eagle*. This particular train began service in 1948 and was actually an extension of the *Texas Eagle* services. However, the *Aztec* and *Texas Eagles* were two separate trains without through equipment, but did operate with the same train numbers 21 and 22. Easy connections were made between the *Texas* and *Aztec Eagles* at San Antonio.

Actually the *Aztec Eagle* was a joint MoPac and National Railways of Mexico train with through Pullmans and coaches between San Antonio and Mexico City. A Missouri Pacific dining-lounge car was also operated between San Antonio and Mexico City.

This arrangement continued through the 1950s. In 1960, the through dining-lounge car was replaced by a MoPac grill-coach between San Antonio and Mexico City. The National Railways of Mexico operated a diner-lounge on the train between Laredo and Mexico City.

Another change came in 1962 when the MP began operating a through St. Louis and Mexico City sleeper on the *Texas Eagle* between St. Louis and San Antonio. South of San Antonio, the *Aztec* carried through coaches to Mexico City while the dining lounge car operated between Nuevo Laredo and Mexico City.

By 1965, the through coaches were discontinued between San Antonio and Mexico, but the sleeping car service continued to operate on the *Texas* and *Aztec Eagles*. Coach passengers were required to change trains at the international border from that time on.

The through sleeper remained in operation into 1969. By 1970, the MoPac no longer provided an *Aztec Eagle* connection, although the National Railways of Mexico continued to operate the train between the U.S.-Mexican border and Mexico City.

AFTER 1970

Although the *Eagle* passenger services disappeared with the coming of Amtrak, the "Eagle" had become a trademark associated with the MP since the 1940s. Not only was the eagle used as part of the motive power paint scheme but the MP even used the name for a fleet of piggyback trains.

In their various forms, the *Eagles* were part of the Missouri Pacific and its territory for nearly 45 years, and were a matter of genuine pride!

The *Louisiana Eagle* arrives at Baton Rouge behind a lone PA in June 1961. (Harold K. Vollrath Collection)

Train 50 meets No. 51 at Eunice, La., in mid-1964. These runs provided daytime service between New Orleans and Houston, and were discontinued in 1965. (J. Parker Lamb)

St. Louis Suburban Service

The Missouri Pacific is generally not thought of as being a commuter or suburban train operator. Although it may be somewhat of a surprise, the MP once operated an extensive fleet of commuter trains between St. Louis, Kirkwood, and Pacific, Missouri. In fact, during the early part of the 1900s, train service was provided on an all-day-long, every-hour basis. As time went on, the service was cut back until by the Depression there were only six Monday-through-Friday runs and four trains on weekends. Patronage continued to fall with increased usage of the automobile until only one pair of MoPac trains continued to serve the St. Louis suburbs by the late 1940s.

The railroad had purchased a small fleet of special high-capacity suburban coaches for use on the St. Louis–Kirkwood–Pacific trains. Originally painted Pullman green, the cars received the *Eagle*

streamliner colors during the early 1950s. The trains were even more attractive in the blue and gray, especially when powered by an Alco road diesel locomotive. In addition to the coaches, at least one combine was part of the fleet. The baggage section was used for the transportation of newpapers and other package business between St. Louis and the suburbs.

The last pair of trains operated on the 34-mile St. Louis–Pacific run were numbered 35 and 36, a daily-except-Saturday, Sunday and Holiday operation. The trains were always included in the system timetable in the St. Louis–Kansas City–Omaha–Lincoln schedules. Because the schedule was so short, it was almost easy to miss trains 35 and 36. After all, one could easily find the *Missouri River* and *Colorado Eagles* in the same timetable, not to mention the other Kansas City and Omaha trains.

Train 35 departed St. Louis after 5:00 p.m. for its one hour, 25 minute run through the western suburbs to Pacific. The train stopped at every station plus a flagstop at Allenton, four miles from Pacific. Inbound, the train departed Pacific after 6:00 a.m. for a nearly 1 hour, 40 minute run to downtown St. Louis. No. 36 had a somewhat softer schedule than the westbound 35. The MoPac timetable always carried an almost superfluous note next to the schedules of 35 and 36: "No checked baggage or remains carried."

During Daylight Savings Time, the MP always adjusted the schedules of trains 35 and 36 to reflect the time in use by the general public. Consequently, during the summer months for example, train 35 departed St. Louis at 4:25 p.m. reflecting a 5:25 departure, which was the case when standard time was in effect. The train departed Pacific at 5:20 a.m. for the actual 6:20

In its final years, with its blue-and-gray cars pulled by a similarly painted diesel, MoPac's St. Louis commuter train resembled a mini-*Eagle*. The commuter train is pausing here at the Kirkwood, Missouri, depot in 1957. Note the streamlined skirts on the coaches. (Dick Wilhelm)

This historic photo shows the last steam locomotive to power a Missouri Pacific commuter train, in 1952. The commuters in this publicity photo at St. Louis seem more interested in the camera. (Missouri Pacific, Author's Collection)

departure. During those days, the railroads were required to print all schedules in "Standard" time because not all states were uniformly on Daylight time during the summer months. Passengers had to adjust, which wasn't always easy and very often trains were missed because of the confusion in times. The Missouri Pacific tried to alleviate this type of problem with advance notices of the time change every April and September, the customary

Daylight time changes prior to the 1960s.

Missouri Pacific trains 35 and 36 were sometimes referred to, unofficially, as the "Little Eagle," with a consist of one locomotive and three or four coaches and a combine for the short-distance commuter run.

The last trip for this very convenient train for commuters and shoppers to and from downtown St. Louis was on December 16, 1961.

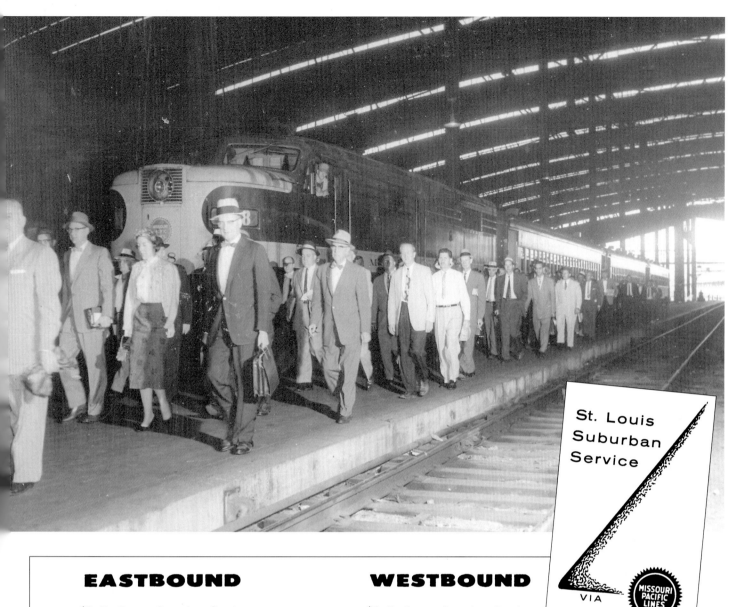

EASTBOUND

*Daily Except Saturday, Sunday
No. 36   and Holidays

Lv. Pacific.	6:20 am
Lv. Eureka.	6:35 am
Lv. Jedburg	6:43 am
Lv. Valley Park	6:55 am
Lv. Barretts	7:05 am
Lv. Kirkwood.	7:15 am
Lv. Woodlawn	7:17 am
Lv. Oakland.	7:18 am
Lv. Glendale.	7:20 am
Lv. Algonquin	7:22 am
Lv. Webster Groves.	7:24 am
Lv. Webster Park.	7:26 am
Lv. Tuxedo Park	7:27 am
Lv. Lake Junction Station . . .	7:29 am
Lv. Edgebrook	. . . . . .
Lv. Maplewood	7:33 am
Lv. Ellendale.	f7:34 am
Ar. Tower Grove	7:39 am
Ar. St. Louis Union Station	7:57 am

WESTBOUND

*Daily Except Saturday, Sunday
No. 35   and Holidays

Lv. St. Louis Union Station.	5:25 pm
Lv. Tower Grove	5:33 pm
Ar. Ellendale.	5:40 pm
Ar. Maplewood	5:41 pm
Ar. Edgebrook	5:43 pm
Ar. Lake Junction Station	f5:45 pm
Ar. Tuxedo Park	5:48 pm
Ar. Webster Park.	5:50 pm
Ar. Webster Groves.	5:52 pm
Ar. Algonquin	5:55 pm
Ar. Glendale	5:57 pm
Ar. Oakland. . . . . :	6:00 pm
Ar. Woodlawn	6:02 pm
Ar. Kirkwood.	6:05 pm
Ar. Barretts	6:12 pm
Ar. Valley Park.	6:17 pm
Ar. Jedburg	6:32 pm
Ar. Eureka	6:38 pm
Ar. Pacific.	6:50 pm

f—flag Stop

***These trains will not operate on Decoration Day, July 4, Labor Day,
Thanksgiving Day, Christmas Day, New Year's Day.***

St. Louis Suburban Service

VIA — MISSOURI PACIFIC LINES

The MoPac's commuter train was one of the only trains to head in to St. Louis Union Station. All other trains backed into the stub-ended terminal upon arrival. During the last years of the commuter train, it was powered by an Alco diesel and the consist was just three suburban coaches. It should be noted, however, that at one time the train did provide baggage service with a combine included in the consist. This photo was taken in 1952. (Missouri Pacific, Author's Collection)

EAGLES IN COLOR

above: Train 106, the *Eagle*, passes Gilmore Junction, Nebraska, on April 17, 1954.

left: The *Missouri River Eagle* at Omaha, Neb., on May 13, 1961. (Both, Lou Schmitz)

above: The *Colorado Eagle* pauses at Kirkwood, Missouri, on June 7, 1959. (Lou Schmitz)

right: The *Eagle*-painted consist of MoPac train No. 110 is powered by steam (4-8-2 No. 5326) as it departs Omaha on November 5, 1950. (Jim Morrison, Lou Schmitz Collection)

below: The *Missourian* at Omaha in July 1951 with a handsome pair of Alco PA's for power. (Jack Pfiefer, Lou Schmitz Collection)

above: Train No. 119, with the 7011 doing the honors, at Gilmore Junction, Nebraska, on April 17, 1954. (Lou Schmitz)

middle: The Missouri Pacific's sole commuter train lays over at Pacific, Missouri, in June 1960. (Richard Wallin, Lou Schmitz Collection)

bottom: Bidirectional AC&F "Motorailer" No. 670, with its coach and baggage-express configuration, served for years as the *Missouri River Eagle* connection between Union and Lincoln, Nebraska. It later was assigned to *Delta Eagle* and other duties. (Lou Schmitz)

opposite top: The early 1960s marked a transition from the blue-and-gray *Eagle* colors to solid blue. The *Missouri River Eagle* departs Omaha through the freight yards and grain elevators with its summer consist of tour cars on July 28, 1963. (Lou Schmitz)

opposite bottom: Train 16, the *Missouri River Eagle*, south of Omaha on June 8, 1963. (Lou Schmitz)

top: Train 17 with a three-car consist at Union, Nebraska, in May 1963. (Dick Rumbolz, Lou Schmitz Collection)

middle: The *Missouri River Eagle* at Omaha on May 13, 1961. Note the stainless steel coach, recently arrived from the Maine Central. (Lou Schmitz)

below: A six-car *Missouri River Eagle* on the prairie north of Fort Crook, Neb., on March 30, 1963. (Lou Schmitz)

opposite top: The combined consist of MoPac Trains 3 and 9 enters El Paso on August 22, 1965, behind E7A No. 2—in solid blue paint but retaining its stainless steel nose eagle. (Kevin J. Holland Collection)

left: By 1965, the *Missouri River Eagle* was handling a substantial amount of head-end business. That was certainly the case on this October 2, 1965, scene which included a Santa Fe baggage car on the head end. A dome coach was still part of the equipment assignments for the *Eagle*. (Lou Schmitz)

above: The Missouri Pacific also handled special campaign trains, such as this four-car Cunningham Special on October 13, 1968. Note the Union Pacific food and beverage cars on the head end. (Lou Schmitz)

right: MoPac Train 22 at Fort Worth on May 29, 1969, two days before the train made its final run. (Tom Hoffmann, Kevin J. Holland Collection)

middle: Missouri Pacific and Texas & Pacific employed these colorful ticket folders, proudly promoting "The Route of the *Eagles*." (Kevin J. Holland Collection)

below: It is the last year of MoPac passenger operations and E8 No. 37 lays over at Kansas City Union Station with an eastbound two-car train for St. Louis. It is July 1970, and Amtrak is just ten months away. (Lou Schmitz Collection)

left: In its last days, the *Missouri River Eagle* typically ran with only two cars. Train 16 paused at Jefferson City, enroute from Kansas City to St. Louis in April 1971, just weeks before Amtrak's debut. (Ron Merrick, Author's Collection)

below: When Amtrak was launched in 1971, it had to rely on the locomotives and rolling stock acquired from its member railroads. Such is the case as Train 15 departs St. Louis on July 11, 1971, still looking very much like a MoPac operation. (Richard Wallin, Lou Schmitz Collection)

above: Milk was served aboard MoPac dining cars in half-pint bottles like this one from Sunnymede Farm of Bismarck, Missouri. (Kevin J. Holland Collection)

above right: These "Special Breakfast" and grill car menu cards employed both the "Buzz Saw" insignia and the dual Missouri Pacific and Texas & Pacific names. (Missouri Pacific, Author's Collection)

right: This ad from MoPac's December 18, 1955, timetable promoted coach service on the *Eagle* fleet. (Kevin J. Holland Collection)

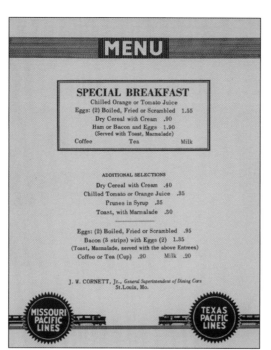

MENU

SPECIAL BREAKFAST
Chilled Orange or Tomato Juice
Eggs: (2) Boiled, Fried or Scrambled 1.55
Dry Cereal with Cream .90
Ham or Bacon and Eggs 1.90
(Served with Toast, Marmalade)

Coffee   Tea   Milk

ADDITIONAL SELECTIONS

Dry Cereal with Cream .40
Chilled Tomato or Orange Juice .35
Prunes in Syrup .35
Toast, with Marmalade .30

Eggs: (2) Boiled, Fried or Scrambled .95
Bacon (3 strips) with Eggs (2) 1.35
(Toast, Marmalade, served with the above Entrees)
Coffee or Tea (Cup) .20   Milk .20

J. W. CORNETT, Jr., *General Superintendent of Dining Cars*
St. Louis, Mo.

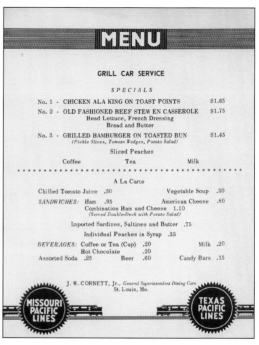

MENU

GRILL CAR SERVICE

SPECIALS

No. 1 - CHICKEN ALA KING ON TOAST POINTS $1.65
No. 2 - OLD FASHIONED BEEF STEW EN CASSEROLE $1.75
Head Lettuce, French Dressing
Bread and Butter

No. 3 - GRILLED HAMBURGER ON TOASTED BUN $1.45
(Pickle Slices, Tomato Wedges, Potato Salad)

Sliced Peaches

Coffee   Tea   Milk

A La Carte

Chilled Tomato Juice .30   Vegetable Soup .30
SANDWICHES: Ham .95   American Cheese .50
Combination Ham and Cheese 1.10
(Served Double-Deck with Potato Salad)
Imported Sardines, Saltines and Butter .75
Individual Peaches in Syrup .35
BEVERAGES: Coffee or Tea (Cup) .20   Milk .20
Hot Chocolate .20
Assorted Soda .25   Beer .60   Candy Bars .15

J. W. CORNETT, Jr., *General Superintendent Dining Cars*
St. Louis, Mo.

RIDE EAGLE COACHES

It's cheaper by far than driving your car! So, why not choose a *soft* and *roomy* reclining-seat on Mo-Pac's ultra-modern EAGLE Coaches? Just relax and laze away the miles . . . arrive refreshed and rested.

★ The TEXAS EAGLES overnight between St. Louis, Memphis and the principal cities of Texas. Through sleeping cars between New York, Washington, Chicago and Texas. *Planetarium-dome coaches* between St. Louis and Dallas, Fort Worth, Austin and San Antonio. Direct connections at Laredo with new streamlined AZTEC EAGLE to Mexico City.

★ The VALLEY EAGLE between Houston, Corpus Christi and the Rio Grande Valley.

★ The COLORADO EAGLE between St. Louis, Kansas City, Wichita and Colorado. *Planetarium-dome coaches* between St. Louis and Denver.

★ The MISSOURI RIVER EAGLE between St. Louis and Kansas City, St. Joseph, Lincoln, Omaha. *Planetarium-dome coaches* between St. Louis and Omaha.

R. J. McDERMOTT
General Passenger Traffic Manager
1601 Missouri Pacific Bldg.
St. Louis 3, Missouri

ROUTE OF THE EAGLES

top: Texas & Pacific E-units were painted in the Missouri Pacific scheme, with only lettering and a T&P diamond in the nose eagle to distinguish them. (Electro-Motive, Kevin J. Holland Collection)

second from top: The MoPac could boast that they operated the most modern express box cars ever constructed, as illustrated by this portrait of No. 163 at Dallas in April 1963. (Lloyd Keyser)

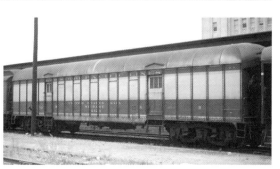

middle left: Texas & Pacific box express car No. 106 in the *Eagle* scheme at Dallas in December 1963. (Lloyd Keyser)

middle right: Baggage car No. 2128 was converted from a mail car —note the narrow doors. It was photographed at Fort Worth in May 1963. (Lloyd Keyser)

bottom: T&P Railway Post Office-baggage car No. 386 in solid blue. (Harry Stegmaier, Jr., Collection)

above: P-S dome coach No. 595. (Harry Stegmaier, Jr., Collection)

middle left: Budd coach No. 467 has lost the fluting below the windows. (Harry Stegmaier, Jr., Collection)

middle right: Coach No. 457. (Harry Stegmaier, Jr., Collection)

second from bottom: After Missouri Pacific acquired the Chicago & Eastern Illinois Railroad, the C&EI's passenger equipment was integrated into the MoPac system. Consequently, C&EI were painted blue with the name in the letter-board and a "Buzz Saw" insignia. Coach 448 (series 444-448 only on MP) illustrates this integration with a blue roof and blue window band and the application of the C&EI Buzz Saw. The car was at Texarkana in 1969. (Ron Merrick)

bottom: P-S coach No. 493 was converted from a MoPac parlor car in the early 1960s, and had been built for the Chesapeake & Ohio in 1950. (Harry Stegmaier, Jr., Collection)

top: *Eagle Cliff* contained 5 double bedrooms and a lounge.

middle left: *Eagle Haven* was one of a group of 10-6 sleepers built by Budd and notable for their six-wheel trucks.

middle right: *Eagle City* was a Texas & Pacific 14 roomette, 4 double bedroom sleeping car.

second from bottom: Missouri Pacific's own fleet of ACF 14-4 sleepers is represented by *Eagle Hill*.

below: Signature cars on the original *Eagles* of 1940 were a pair of round-ended observation cars, complete with cast-aluminum eagles. No. 750 is preserved at the National Museum of Transport in St. Louis. (All, (Harry Stegmaier, Jr., Collection)

AMTRAK ON THE MISSOURI PACIFIC

The Missouri Pacific Railroad was (and is within the Union Pacific) one of the major railroads operating Amtrak passenger trains. The MoPac was part of the Amtrak system immediately on May 1, 1971. A through train between New York and Kansas City was placed in operation by Amtrak. Numbered 15 and 16, the train utilized the MP between St. Louis and Kansas City. The train provided sleeping, coach and dining-lounge services. By November 14, 1971, the train was designated the *National Limited* and renumbered 30 and 31. Those numbers were also used by the MoPac during the train's operation over the 283-mile Sedalia Subdivision of the Northern Division.

Trains 30 and 31 were eventually re-equipped with Amfleet coach and dinette equipment and rebuilt sleepers utilizing head-end power (HEP). The train was finally discontinued on October 1,

above: Amtrak SDP40F No. 618 waits in a sand storm as it prepares to depart with Train 22, the *Inter-American*, from the MoPac station in Laredo, Texas, on March 11, 1977. The consist of No. 22 includes a sleeping car, lounge car, two coaches and a baggage-dormitory car. (J. W. Swanberg)

left: The Kirkwood, Missouri, station includes a sign with the Amtrak insignia. (Thomas Dorin)

below: The eastbound *National Limited* departs the St. Louis suburb of Kirkwood on June 28, 1972. (A. Robert Johnson, Author's Collection)

1979, and replaced by the *Ann Rutledge*, a through Amfleet consist between Chicago and Kansas City on a daytime schedule. In fact, as of the winter of 2002, the *Ann Rutledge* still operated over the Chicago–Kansas City routing as trains 303-304.

The second Amtrak train to grace MoPac rails was the *Inter-American*, launched as trains 21 and 22 between Fort Worth and Laredo, Texas, in April 1973. The schedule was extended to a St. Louis–Laredo service in 1974 on a tri-weekly basis. Two years later, in October 1976, the *Inter-American* began operating as a through Chicago–Laredo train with daily service between Chicago and Fort Worth and tri-weekly beyond. In June 1977 the train was placed on a daily schedule for the entire Chicago–Laredo route.

During the fall of 1980 train service was doubled between St. Louis and Kansas City. Amtrak added the *St.*

Louis Mule and the *Kansas City Mule*, numbers 32 and 33 on the MoPac (Amtrak numbers 342 and 341, respectively). With the addition of the two new trains, service into and out of St. Louis was the most extensive it had been since the late 1960s.

During the summer of 1981, Amtrak re-equipped the *Inter-American* with new Superliner equipment. This was a major and significant change, and was a welcome addition on this long-distance train. Other changes in the early 1980s saw the discontiuance of the *Inter-American* between San Antonio and Laredo. At the same time, the train was renamed the *Eagle* over the remainder of its run.

Moving into the first decade of the 21st century, Amtrak operates the *Texas Eagle* as a tri-weekly train between St. Louis and San Antonio, with through Chicago–Los Angeles coaches and sleeping cars. The *Texas Eagle* operates daily between Chicago and St. Louis over former GM&O trackage.

There are two sets of trains in each direction on the St. Louis–Kansas City route—the *Ann Rutledge* and the *St. Louis Mule* and *Kansas City Mule*, trains 303 and 304; and 306 and 301, respectively.

In May 2001 Amtrak marked the completion of three decades of service over MoPac rails, which are now, of course, part of the Union Pacific Railroad system.

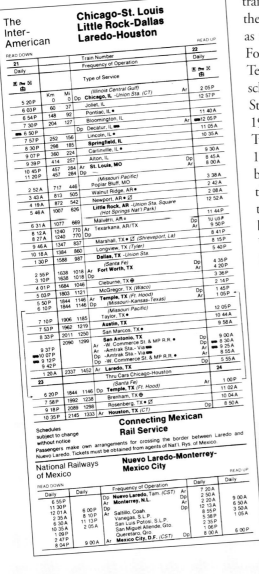

The *Inter-American* was re-equipped with Amfleet cars and F40PH locomotives in the mid-1970s. However, in the case of Trains 21 and 22, there was a combination of Amfleet and "Heritage Fleet" equipment converted for head-end power. Such was the case as train 21 arrives in St. Louis (from Chicago) with eight cars destined for Texas points. At St. Louis, the MP took over the train for most of the run to the Mexican border at Laredo. This photo was taken in May 1980. (Author)

Amtrak train No. 304, running as MP train 30, has just arrived at the St. Louis depot in May 1980. The train is en route from Kansas City to Chicago via St. Louis. Additonal St. Louis and Kansas City service is provided by the *St. Louis Mule* and *Kansas City Mule*, giving the "Show Me" state a double-daily schedule in both directions. (Author)

Amtrak trains sometimes need freight railroad motive power to fill in or provide extra horsepower. In this case Train 22, the Superliner-equipped *Inter-American*, is headed up by MoPac GE B23-7 No. 4518 and two Amtrak F40PH's on June 13, 1981. In October 1981, the *Inter-American* name was dropped in favor of a new—and former MoPac—name, the *Eagle*. Later the train would receive the full name as the *Texas Eagle*. (Jim Bennett)

HEAD-END EQUIPMENT

Head-end business—the mail and express traffic handled, typically, at the front of passenger trains—provided a substantial amount of the passenger revenue over the many decades of MoPac operations. This was especially true in the latter years.

The Missouri Pacific operated some rather interesting pieces of head-end equipment. One could find not only standard and streamlined head-end cars, but also heavyweight, outside-braced cars unique to the MoPac. The photogaphs and diagrams on the following pages illustrate part of this fleet of cars that in many cases added years to the life of various MoPac passenger trains.

Many of the diagrams included in this chapter show both a particular car's original number and subsequent renumberings. In some cases, the diagrams show that the cars were actually renumbered twice.

above: Loading of mail and express complete, the *Texas Eagle* is ready to depart Houston in this 1948 view. (Kevin J. Holland Collection)

left: MoPac Northern No. 2208 leads a head-end-heavy train out of St. Louis Union Station in 1950. Note the PRR express box car. (Railroad Avenue Enterprises Collection)

above: A fleet of 50-foot, double-door box cars with high-speed trucks was built by MP's Sedalia shops. Cars were Pullman green with gold lettering. (Missouri Pacific, Author's Collection)

middle and below: MP built 70-foot, double-door mail storage cars, painted blue with a gray stripe and numbered 135 to 184. (Author's Collection)

top: MP baggage car 2059 illustates the standard "monitor" or clerestory roof. The company had designated this series for U.S. Mail storage and appropriate lettering was applied between the doors. Car numbers were placed above the trucks.

above: Baggage car 4208 operated in express service with the lettering "Railway Express Agency." Note the placement of "Missouri Pacific Lines" as well as the initials "MP."

middle: Arch-roof baggage car 4256 had welded sides and was assigned to the Railway Express Agency. (Three views, Missouri Pacific, Author's Collection)

bottom: T&P baggage-express car 835 in *Eagle* colors. (Marsh-Williams Collection)

above: This heavy-weight MoPac baggage-express car still wore classic *Eagle* colors in 1970. (Marsh-Williams Collection)

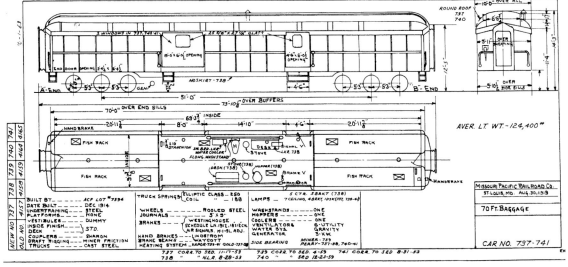

middle: Diagram of baggage car series 737 to 741 after renumbering. (Missouri Pacific, Author's Collection)

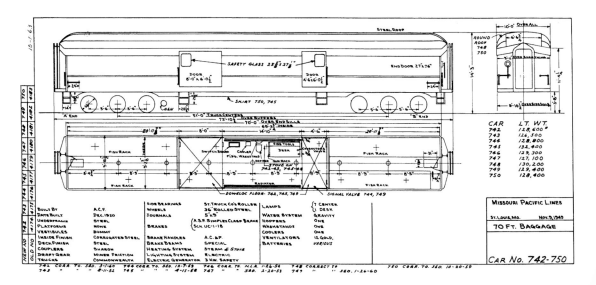

bottom: Baggage car series 742 to 750 was also in the 70-foot category. Two cars in this group were equipped with skirts, Nos. 745 and 750. (Missouri Pacific, Author's Collection)

top: MoPac No. 233 at Ft. Worth. (Marsh-Williams Collection)

second from top: Streamlined baggage car 277 (series 250 to 299) was an 85-foot car, and finished its days in the solid blue with a gray stripe and one bright red MP insignia in the car center. This car was photographed during the layover for Trains 54 and 55 at Brownsville, Texas in June 1965. (Ralph Carlson)

second from bottom: Streamlined baggage car 288 served as a mail storage car for most of its operating career. (William A. Raia Collection)

bottom: After Amtrak, many MoPac baggage cars were reassigned as work equipment or used for storage. Such is the case with car 271, photographed in December 1980. (Dennis Roos)

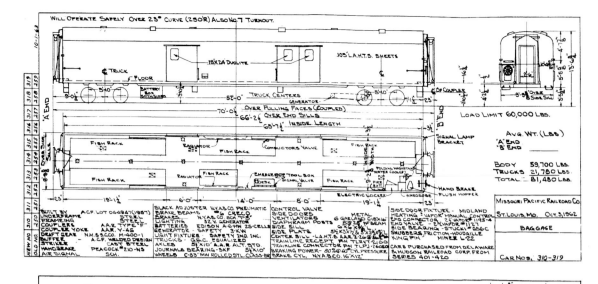

The MoPac operated an extensive fleet of 70-foot streamlined baggage cars such as the 310-319 series. An interesting piece of information from this diagram is that this group of cars could operate over 23 degree curves and No. 7 switches. (Missouri Pacific, Author's Collection)

One example of the *Eagle* streamlined baggage cars is the series 352-354. These cars were built in 1942 and operated on two sets of the early *Eagles*. (Missouri Pacific, Author's Collection)

The Missouri Pacific invested in a number of head-end cars with outside bracing. This "Sullivan-Renshaw" design—Railway Post Office car 2129 (series 2110 to 2130)—was purchased from American Car & Foundry in 1911. The car was 64 feet, 6 inches long. (Missouri Pacific, Author's Collection)

RPO car 2302 was one of three cars in its class (2301 to 2303) and was once referred to as a "Fast Mail Letter Car." It was 64 feet, 7 inches long. Note the MP initials in the upper corners, but in this case the car carries only the words, "Missouri Pacific." (Missouri Pacific, Author's Collection)

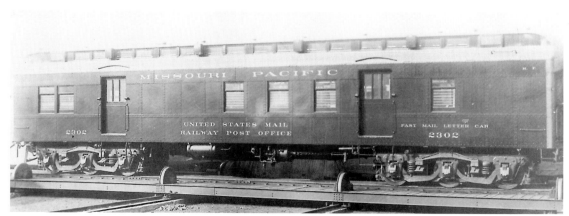

top: RPO 2140 (Marsh-Williams Collection)

middle: Railway Post Office car 2581 (series 2571 to 2587) represents the most typical type of combination mail and baggage cars found throughout North America, with its 30-foot post office "apartment." The car was photographed in service on trains 54 and 55 while laying over in Brownsville, Texas, on April 22, 1963. Dressed in blue, the car has probably seen its last overhaul and new paint. The end of service was not that far away. Note that with the new blue scheme, the car carries only the insignia for lettering. The number is placed between the baggage door and the end of the car. (Ralph Carlson)

bottom: RPO-baggage No. 1018, at Brownsville in August 1965, reflects a semi-streamlined version of the typical RPO configuration. Note the smooth roof lines and lack of rivets. (Ralph Carlson)

One rather impressive Railway Post Office car design was the 60-foot variety, devoted exclusively to mail service. MoPac car No. 1041 was part of the 1040-1051 series, ex- 2131-2142. Note the six-wheel trucks, rare for a light-weight car.

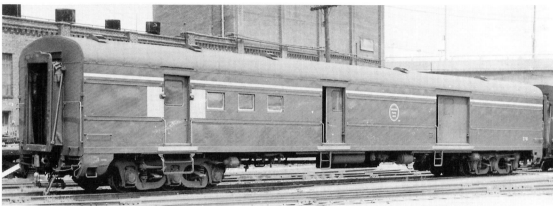

RPO-Baggage No. 376 (374-376, 378, 381) was equipped with three sets of doors on each side. Again, this streamlined, light-weight car rode on "classic" six-wheel trucks. (Both, William A. Raia Collection)

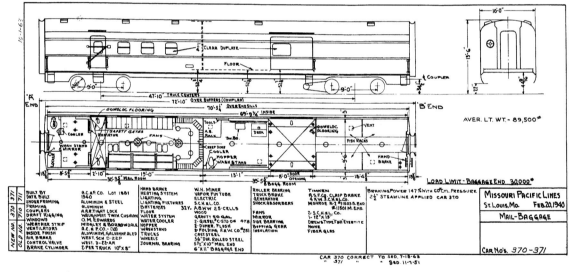

RPO-Baggage cars 370 and 371 were originally built for service on the *Eagle*. The cars are 72 feet, 10 inches long over buffers. (Missouri Pacific, Author's Collection)

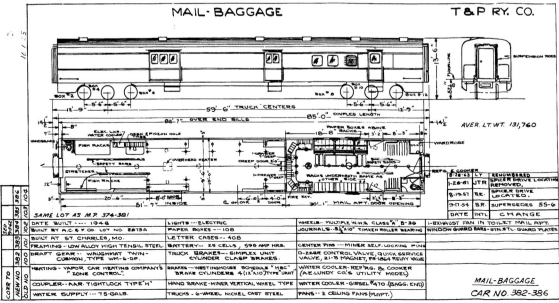

Streamlined baggage cars 382-386 were part of the Texas & Pacific Railway fleet, which of course operated in conjunction with through train services over the MoPac. (Missouri Pacific, Author's Collection)

82

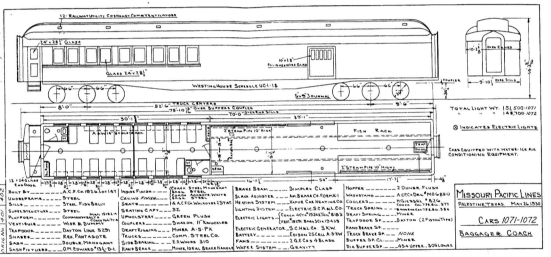

top: Texas & Pacific baggage car 383 is a former RPO-baggage car. (William A. Raia Collection)

middle: Cars 1071-1072 were air-conditioned and operated in mainline service. (Jim Bennett Collection)

below: Baggage-dorm No. 365 provided crew accommodations for the *Texas Eagle* and other trains. (MoPac, Author's Collection)

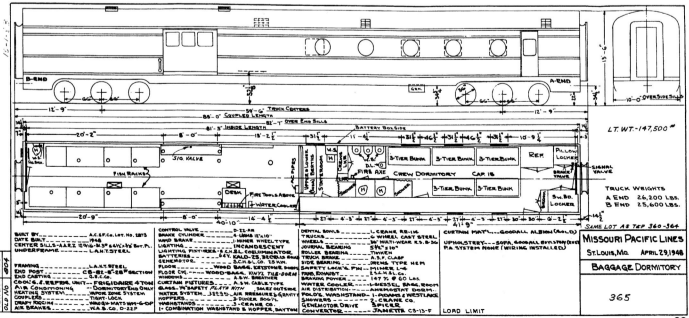

above: Note the semi-streamlined skirts at the ends of 73-foot standard baggage car No. 786. (William A. Raia Collection)

middle: Standard baggage cars, such as 986 (983-987) also received the final blue color scheme. (William A. Raia Collection)

below: T&P baggage car No. 360 was an 85-foot car riding on six-wheel trucks. The insignia includes "TP" initials. (William A. Raia Collection)

MISSOURI PACIFIC LINES
HEAD-END EQUIPMENT ROSTER (1963 RENUMBERING)

Railroad	Type	Series	Former Series	Length	Railroad	Type	Series	Former Series	Length
T&P	Box Express	100-124	1700-1724	41' 9"	MP	Mail Storage	955-956	2041-2042	73' 9"
MP	RPO-Baggage	112-113 115	(Ex-IGN)	74' 2"	MP	Mail Storage	957-958	2043-2044	82' 4"
MP	Coach-RPO	126-127	61-62		MP	Mail Storage	959-968	2050-2059	73' 6"
MP	Box Express	135-184	135-184	73' 9"	MP	Mail Storage	969-970	2060-2061	78' 7"
MP	Mail Storage	200-249		85'	MP	Mail Storage	971	2066	76' 10"
MP	Mail Storage	250-299		85'	MP	Mail Storage	972	2068	81' 7"
MP	Baggage	310-319	250-259	70' 7"	MP	Mail Storage	973-974	2072-2073	81' 7"
MP	Baggage	351	701	73' 4"	MP	Mail Storage	975	2074	
MP	Baggage	352-354	702-704	73' 8"	MP	Mail Storage	976	2075	82' 4"
T&P	Baggage Dorm.	360-361 363-364	300-304	85' 6"	MP	Mail Storage	977	2126	64' 6"
MP	Baggage Dorm.	365	804	85' 6"	MP	Mail Storage	978	2301	
MP	Box Express	370-371	710-711	73' 4"	MP	Mail Storage	979	2554	73' 10"
MP	RPO-Baggage	372-373	712-713	73' 8"	MP	Mail Storage	980	2557	73' 10"
MP	RPO-Baggage	374-376 378, 381	810-817	85' 6"	MP	Mail Storage	981-982	2588-2589	73' 10"
T&P	Baggage	382-386	100-104	85'	MP	Mail Storage	983-987	4169-4173	73' 10"
MP	Baggage	700	121	74' 1"	T&P	Mail Storage	988-989	1180-1181	
MP	Baggage	701-715	198-212		T&P	Mail Storage	990	618	62'
MP	Baggage	716-722	222-228		T&P	Mail Storage	991	623	62'
MP	Baggage	723-735	4151-4154	74' 0"	T&P	Mail Storage	992	627	62'
MP	Baggage	736-739	4156-4159	73' 11"	T&P	Mail Storage	993	639	62'
MP	Baggage	740-741	4164-4165	73' 11"	T&P	Mail Storage	994	624	62'
MP	Baggage	742-745	4174-4177	73' 11"	T&P	Mail Storage	995-996	631-632	62'
MP	Baggage	746-750	4179-4183	73' 11"	T&P	Mail Storage	997	636	62'
MP	Baggage	751-807	4185-4242	73' 11"	T&P	Mail Storage	998	638	62'
MP	Baggage	808 809-814	4244 4246-4251	73' 11"	T&P	Mail Storage	999	1124	72' 3"
MP	Baggage	815-819	4255-4259	78' 7"	MP	RPO-Baggage	1000	112	74' 2"
MP	Baggage	820-826	4261-4267	78' 7"	MP	RPO-Baggage	1001	115	74' 2"
MP	Baggage	827-831	4268-4272	78' 4"	MP	RPO-Baggage	1002	116	74' 2"
T&P	Baggage	832-833	621-622	62'	MP	RPO-Baggage	1003-1004	123-124	73' 10"
T&P	Baggage	834	624	62'	MP	RPO-Baggage	1005	2551	73' 10"
T&P	Baggage	835	628	62'	MP	RPO-Baggage	1006	2559	73' 1"
T&P	Baggage	836-838	630-632	62'	MP	RPO-Baggage	1007	2562	73' 1"
T&P	Baggage	839-841	634-636	62'	MP	RPO-Baggage	1008-1011	2564-2567	73' 1"
T&P	Baggage	842	638	62'	MP	RPO-Baggage	1012-1013	2569-2570	73' 1"
T&P	Baggage	843-846	650-653	62'	MP	RPO-Baggage	1014-1018	2571-2575	73' 10"
T&P	Baggage	847-878	1101-1132	72' 3"	MP	RPO-Baggage	1019-1024	2577-2582	73' 10"
T&P	Baggage	879-883	1150-1154	78'	MP	RPO-Baggage	1025-1028	2584-2587	73' 10"
T&P	Baggage	884-889	1155-1160		T&P	RPO-Baggage	1030	903	73'
T&P	Baggage	890-894	1170-1174		T&P	RPO-Baggage	1031	905	73'
T&P	Baggage	895-895	1180-1181		T&P	RPO-Baggage	1032	907	73'
MP	Mail Storage	930	2006	64' 6"	T&P	RPO-Baggage	1033	910	73'
MP	Mail Storage	931-934	2008-2011	64' 6"	T&P	RPO-Baggage	1034-1038	912-916	73'
MP	Mail Storage	935	2016	64' 6"	MP	RPO	1040-1051	2131-2142	64' 6"
MP	Mail Storage	936	2018	64' 6"	MP	RPO	1052-1055	715-718	63'
MP	Mail Storage	937	2021	64' 6"	MP	RPO-44-seat Coach	1066-1067	126-127	75' 11"
MP	Mail Storage	938-945	2022-2029	82' 5"	MP	Bag.-32-seat Coach	1071-1072	131-132	75' 11"
MP	Mail Storage	946-949	2031-2034	82' 5"	MP	Bag.-30-seat Coach	1073-1074 1075	3611-3612 3618	76' 6"
MP	Mail Storage	950	2035	82' 4"					
MP	Mail Storage	951-952	2036-2037	71' 1"	MP	Trailer Flat (Mail)	990002, 990004 990017, 990018		89' 1"
MP	Mail Storage	953	2038	78' 4"			999995-999999		94' 2"
MP	Mail Storage	954	2039	75' 3"					

8

COACHES AND
PARLOR CARS

Depending upon the type of train, the coach or chair car provided the basic service for travel from one point to another. Missouri Pacific's standard heavyweight coaches provided seating for up to 80 (and sometimes more) passengers while the newer streamlined cars could handle up to 72 passengers. Parlor cars, on the other hand, typically sat up to 30 passengers.

This chapter illustrates the various types of MoPac coaches, including the dome coaches and various combination cars such coach-dormitories, coach-parlor cars, full parlor cars, and parlor observation cars. The diagrams provide additional technical information including car number changes, opposite-side window configurations, and other data.

It is safe to say that the Missouri Pacific had some of the finest coach and parlor car equipment ever designed.

above: The parlor observation car was superb punctuation for the *Missouri River Eagle*. The original six-car consist included two coaches, seating 132 passengers (56 in the long-distance car and 76 in the local coach) plus 26 seats in the parlor car. Total revenue space was 158 seats, plus a six-seat lounge in the rear of the parlor car.

left: Interior view of a MoPac Pullman-Standard dome, looking toward the rear and down the stairs to the lower level. (Both, Missouri Pacific, Author's Collection)

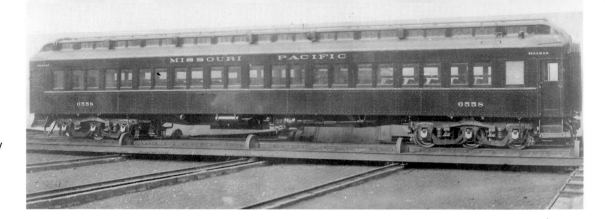

top: St. Louis, Iron Mountain & Southern 80-seat coach 6558 was built by AC&F in February 1915.

second from top: A more modern MoPac coach is illustrated by St. Louis, Brownsville & Mexico No. 445. In the case the word "Chair" describes the long-distance service assignments for this equipment.

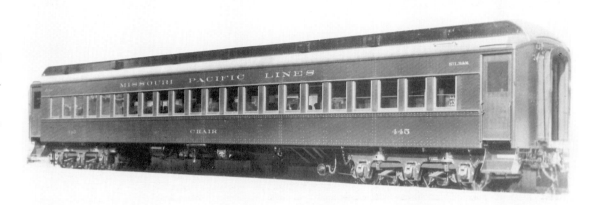

second from bottom: Coach 6409 was one of a kind and reflected some minor modifications including a semi-skirt.

bottom: 52-seat coach 6309 (series 6309 to 6310) reflects further rebuilding of a standard coach into a semi-streamlined car. (All, Missouri Pacific, Author's Collection)

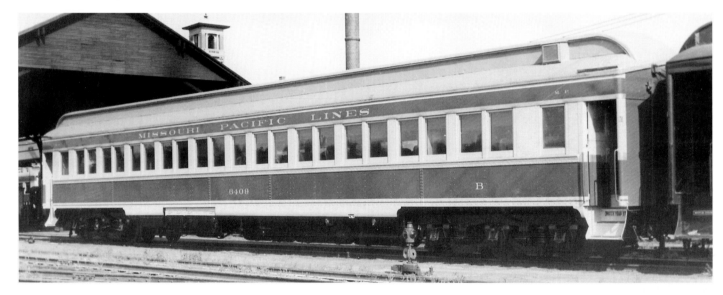

top: T&P coach 1139 (series 1133-1140), at Brownsville, Texas, in June 1965, has been modernized as a semi-streamlined car, with picture windows and welded sides. The car continued to ride on six-wheel trucks. Note the retention of vestibules at both ends. (Ralph Carlson)

left: Streamlined coach 477 (ex-730) reflects the rebuilding and modernization process, minus skirts, at Brownsville on February 1, 1965. (Ralph Carlson)

second from bottom: Coach No. 466, the former 861, had lost its *Eagle* paint scheme and lettering when this photograph was taken in 1965. Although repainted, the car retained the fluted sides, roof, and skirting. (Ralph Carlson)

bottom: Budd coach 483 (482-483, ex-771-772) could seat 56 passengers. (William A. Raia Collection)

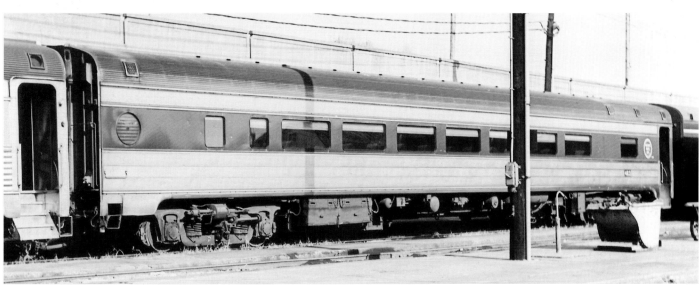

above: *Eagle* coach 770 was part of series 770-777 built in 1947 by P-S. These coaches were purchased from the Maine Central in 1960 and lacked the characteristic MoPac porthole windows. (Missouri Pacific, Author's Collection)

second from top: Coach 425 was originally built by Budd as a 48-seat grill-coach for the *Colorado Eagle*. The car was rebuilt in the 1960s with additional windows in a full coach configuration. The original number was 723, later 525, and finally 425. (Missouri Pacific, Author's Collection)

second from bottom: Diagram for dormitory coach No. 524. (Missouri Pacific, Author's Collection)

bottom: Dormitory coach No. 524 was built by the Budd Company in 1942 as a grill-coach for the *Colorado Eagle*. The original number was 722 (with sister car 723). Both cars were converted from grill-coach configuration to dormitory coaches in 1959. Seating capacity was reduced from 48 seats to 40. The dormitory section could accommodate 15 crewmen in five sections of three-tier bunks. Car 722 became 524 in 1963. (Missouri Pacific, Author's Collection)

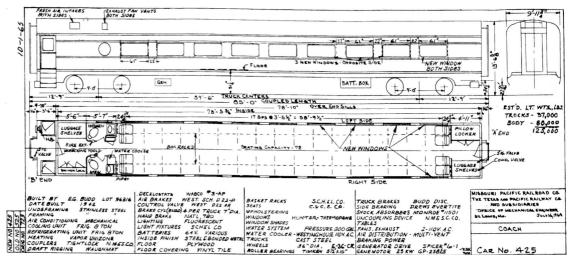

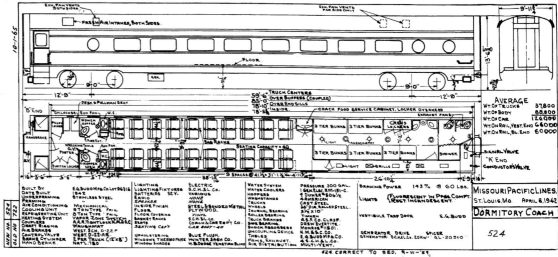

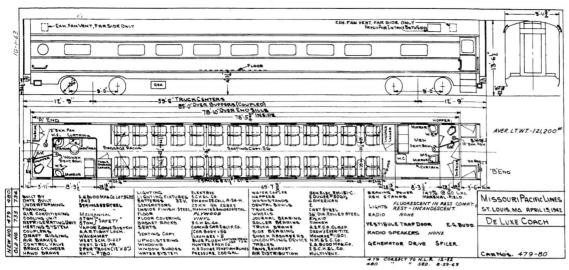
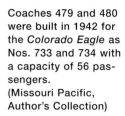

Coaches 479 and 480 were built in 1942 for the *Colorado Eagle* as Nos. 733 and 734 with a capacity of 56 passengers. (Missouri Pacific, Author's Collection)

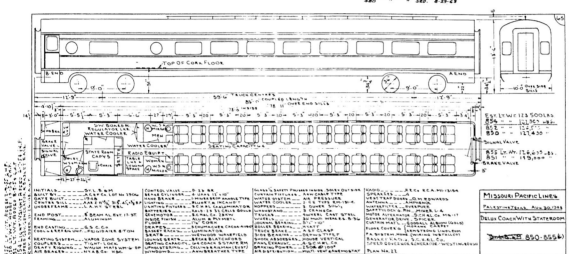

Among the most unusual *Eagle* coaches built were the Stateroom (another name for drawing room) cars, series 850 to 855. Built for the St. Louis, Brownsville & Mexico Railroad, the cars contained observation windows. The group was built by American Car & Foundry in 1948. (Missouri Pacific, Author's Collection)

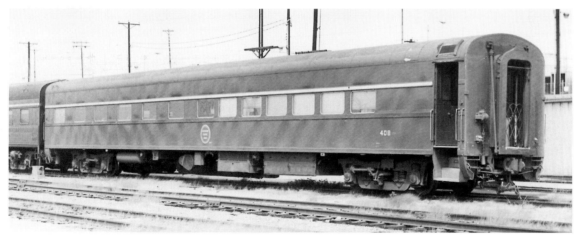

Coach 408 was a rebuilt sleeping car with 76 seats. It was the former *Eagle Glide*, a 14-2-1 Pullman car. (William A. Raia Collection)

Coach 404 was another MoPac sleeping car rebuilt as a coach. In this case, the *Eagle Circle* lost its interior to 76 coach seats. (William A. Raia Collection)

above: Pullman-Standard built four dome coaches for the Missouri Pacific and one for the Texas & Pacific in 1952. They were originally numbered 893-896 and T&P 200, renumbered in 1963 to 593-597. The five dome cars were purchased for service on the Texas Eagles and remained in that service until 1967. All carried 42 revenue seats except for 593 which contained 52 seats. All were sold to the Illinois Central in 1967 except for 593 which had been retired in 1967. Car 896 was sublettered for the International-Great Northern, a MoPac subsidiary. (Missouri Pacific, Author's Collection)

middle: Diagram plan for the dome car 593. (Missouri Pacific, Author's Collection)

bottom: The interior of the Pullman-Standard domes for the MoPac *Texas Eagles* looking toward the stairway to the dome. Note the location of the water cooler in front of the coach seats to the right of the stairway. (Missouri Pacific, Author's Collection)

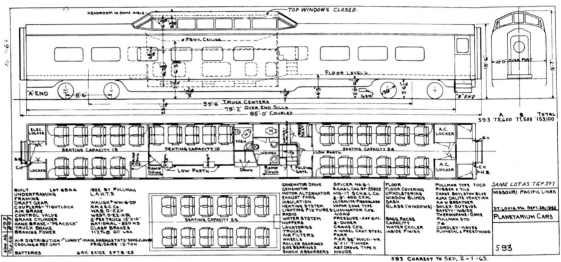

left: Interior view of the Budd dome looking toward the rear of the car and down the steps to the lower level. Note the contrast to the angular design of the Pullman-Standard domes (see photo on page 87). (Missouri Pacific, Author's Collection)

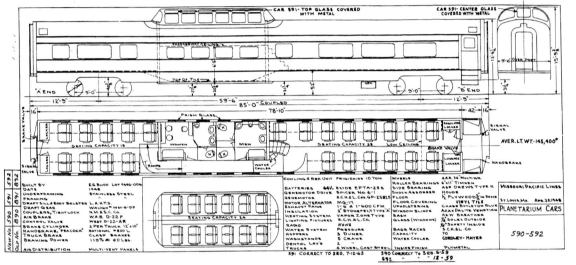

middle: Diagram of the Budd-built dome coaches, 590 to 592. (Missouri Pacific, Author's Collection)

below: Dome coach No. 890, lettered for the *Colorado Eagle*, was photographed in service on the *Missouri River Eagle* at Omaha in 1955. (Harold Ranks, Lou Schmitz Collection)

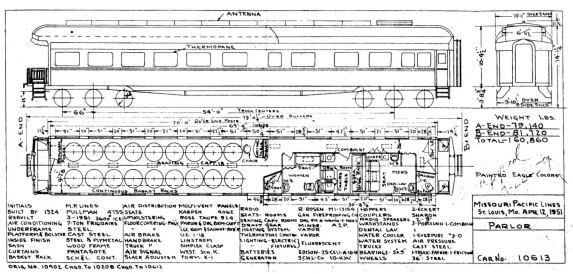

top: One of the more distinctive types of MoPac parlor cars were those with open-end observation platforms like No. 10613. Originally numbered 10902, it was renumbered to 10208 before becoming the 10613. This car was painted in the *Eagle* colors. (Missouri Pacific, Jim Bennett Colection)

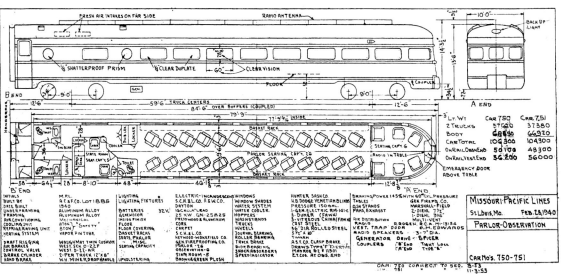

middle: Two extraordinary streamlined parlor observation cars were built by AC&F for the *Missouri River Eagle* in 1940. (Missouri Pacific, Jim Bennett Collection)

bottom: The interiors of the *Missouri River Eagle* parlor observation cars were equipped with swivel, reclining lounge chairs. This view shows the interior looking toward the observation room. (Missouri Pacific, Author's Collection)

MISSOURI PACIFIC LINES
COACH AND PARLOR CAR ROSTER (1963 RENUMBERING)

Railroad	Type	Series	Former Series	Notes	Railroad	Type	Series	Former Series	Notes
MP	Parlor	87-88	754-755		MP	Coach	1105	6168	70 seats
MP	Coach	345-346	144-145		MP	Coach	1106		
MP	Coach	400-401	720-721		MP	Coach	1107		
MP	Coach	402	Eagle Bridge	Rebuilt Sleeper	MP	Coach	1108		
MP	Coach	403	Eagle Village	Rebuilt Sleeper	MP	Coach	1109		
MP	Coach	404	Eagle Circle	Rebuilt Sleeper	MP	Coach	1110		
MP	Coach	405	Eagle Flight	Rebuilt Sleeper	MP	Coach	1111		
MP	Coach	406	Eagle County	Rebuilt Sleeper	MP	Coach	1112		
T&P	Coach	407	Eagle Watch	Rebuilt Sleeper	MP	Coach	1113		
MP	Coach	408	Eagle Glide	Rebuilt Sleeper	MP	Coach	1114		
T&P	Coach	409	Eagle Trail	Rebuilt Sleeper	MP	Coach	1115		
MP	Coach	410	Eagle Creek	Rebuilt Sleeper	MP	Coach	1116		
MP	Coach	411	Eagle Rock	Rebuilt Sleeper	MP	Coach	1117-1121	6306-6310	52 seats
IGN	Coach	425-426	227-228	72 seats	MP	Coach	1122-1123	6332-6333	56 seats
IGN	Coach	429-432		62 seats	MP	Coach	1124	8153	70 seats
T&P	Coach	450-461		60 seats	T&P	Coach	1125-1132	1650-1657	52 seats
MP	Coach	462-464	831-833	60 seats; ex-IGN	T&P	Coach	1133-1140	1658-1665	
MP	Coach	465-474	860-869	64 seats	T&P	Coach	1141-1149	1675-1685	56 seats
T&P	Coach	475-476	400-401	64 seats	IGN	Coach	1160-1161	337-338	60 seats
MP	Coach	477-478	730-731	61 seats	CGL	Coach	1162-1163	443-444	60 seats; (StLB&M)
MP	Coach	481	770	72 seats	CGL	Coach	1164-1165	448-449	60 seats; (StLB&M)
MP	Coach	482-483	771-772	56 seats	MP	Coach	1166	6165	70 seats
MP	Coach	484	773	72 seats	MP	Coach	1167	6171	70 seats
MP	Coach	485-488	774-777	56 seats	MP	Coach	1168	6174	72 seats
MP	Coach	489	830	60 seats	MP	Coach	1169	6179	70 seats
MP	Coach	490-493	750-753	60 seats	MP	Coach	1170-1171	6181-6182	76 seats
MP	Coach	494-499	850-855	64 seats	MP	Coach	1172	6184	76 seats
MP	Co-Dorm	520-523	820-823	52 seats	MP	Coach	1173	6188	76 seats
MP	Co-Dorm	524-525	722-723	48 seats	MP	Coach	1174	6191	76 seats
MP	Dome	590-592	890-892	70 seats	MP	Coach	1175	6199	70 seats
MP	Dome	593-595	893-896	81 seats	MP	Coach	1176	6406	76 seats
T&P	Dome	597	200	81 seats	MP	Coach	1177	6551	84 seats
MP	Coach	1094	6312		MP	Coach	1178	6558	80 seats
MP	Coach	1095	6313		MP	Coach	1180	6561	60 seats
MP	Coach	1097	345		MP	Coach	1181-1187	6562-6568	60 seats
MP	Coach	1098	346		MP	Coach	1188	6570	60 seats
MP	Coach	1099	6176	70 seats	MP	Coach	1189	6573	68 seats
IGN	Coach	1100	336	52 seats	MP	Coach	1190	6575	60 seats
GCL	Coach	1101-1103	445-447	52 seats; (StLB&M)	MP	Coach	1191-1192	10303-10304	64 seats; ex-IGN
MP	Coach	1104	6151	70 seats					

MoPac operated four parlor cars, series 752 to 755, which had been purchased from the Chesapeake & Ohio in March 1959. Between 1962 and 1964, they were converted to 60-seat coaches. Car 752, shown here, was the first to be converted and renumbered 490 in October 1962. (Missouri Pacific, Author's Collection)

DINING AND
LOUNGE CARS

The Missouri Pacific operated a variety of dining, lounge, and combination cars with such designations as diner-lounge, grill-coach, cafe-coach-parlor, dining-parlor, cafe coach, and observation cars.

This chapter reviews part of this fleet, which almost deserves a book of its own, as well as menus and recipes.

above: MoPac rebuilt a number of dining cars into diner-lounges (10230-10235) with rich interiors.

left: Dining Club car 10223 was built in 1930 and provided dining, parlor, and lounge service. (Both, Missouri Pacific, Author's Collection)

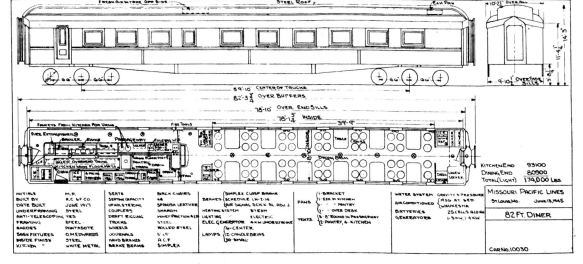

top: MoPac diner No. 10030 was built by American Car & Foundry in 1917. This diagram shows the car as originally built. (Missouri Pacific, Author's Collection)

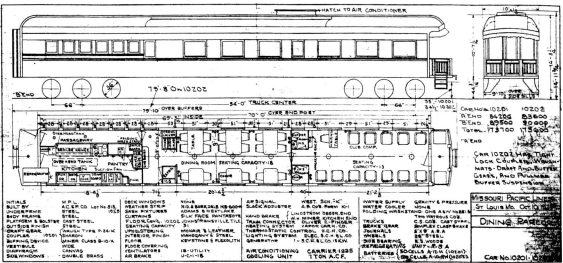

middle: Diagram of MoPac dining parlor cars 10201 and 10202 illustrates the parlor section and the 18-seat dining room in the center of these dining-parlor cars. (Missouri Pacific, Jim Bennett Collection)

below: Cars 10201 and 10202 provided dining and parlor car service as well as the classic open-end observation. (Missouri Pacific, Author's Collection)

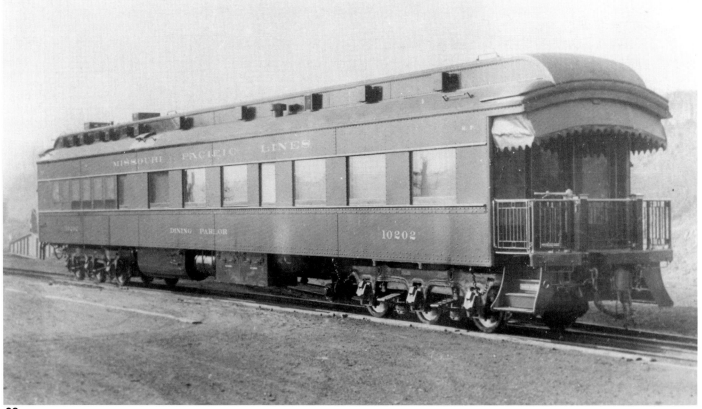

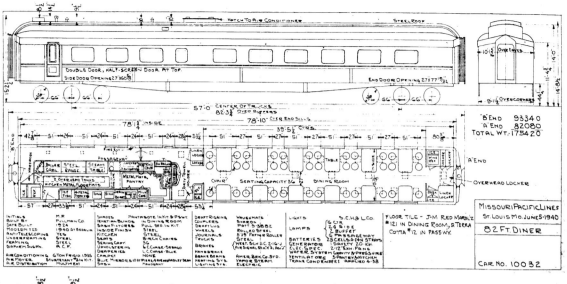

top: Dining car No. 10032 was built by Pullman in 1924 and reflects a number of changes in the basic car design. One of the interesting changes was the style of window, even though their arrangement and placement remained the same. The windows were streamlined and sealed for air conditioning. (Missouri Pacific, Jim Bennett Collection)

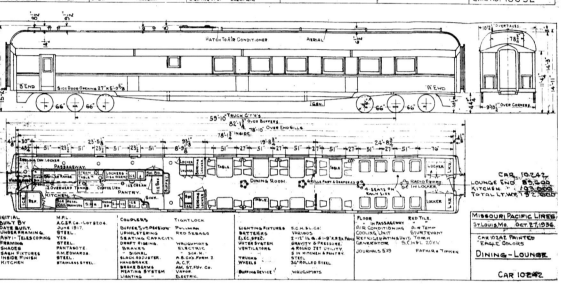

second from top: Dining-lounge car 10242 reflects a change in the window configuration on the kitchen side for this car, which was built in 1917 by AC&F. There was a complete change in the roof as well as the addition of skirting. Cars 10241 and 10242 (the former 10029 and 10027 respectively), were painted in the *Eagle* color scheme. (Missouri Pacific, Jim Bennett Collection)

second from bottom: Dining car 10239, *Queretaro*, closely resembles the diagram of dining car 10242. There are differences with the roof and air conditioning duct. Note the complete change in the window configuration in the kitchen area. (W. C. Whittaker Collection)

bottom: MoPac No. 10238, a sister to the car in the upper photo, showing the opposite-side window arrangement. (Harry Stegmaier, Jr., Collection)

top: This diagram illustrates still another type of combination meal and revenue service equipment operated by the Missouri Pacific Lines. Cars 10904 and 10905 carried the the M.P. intials and had a cafe-coach interior configuration with coach seating at both the forward and rear of the car. The drawing also indicates that there were windows in the rear bulk head. The center dining room provided seating for 16 passengers. (Missouri Pacific, Jim Bennett Collection)

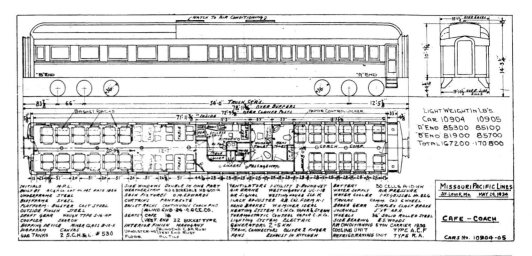

second from top: Coach-cafe-parlor No. 10906 was truly an interesting car with three different types of accommodations and services. The rear section contained 10 parlor seats instead of the coach seating found in the cafe-coach. Again we have windows to the rear of the car creating an observation room, which was very practical with the rotating parlor seats. The car was painted in the *Eagle* colors. (Missouri Pacific, Jim Bennett Collection)

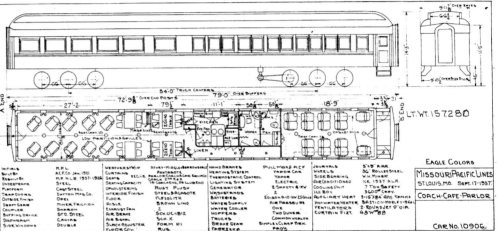

second from bottom: Lounge cars 10303 and 10304 were built by Pullman in 1927. The cars carried the initials I-GN for the International-Great Northern, a MoPac subsidiary. (Missouri Pacific, Jim Bennett Collection)

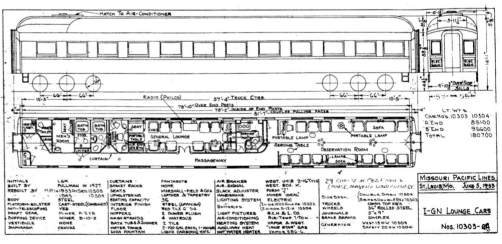

bottom: Lounge cars 10301 and 10302 were built by Pullman in 1930. They were comparable to Nos. 10303 and 10304, but with additional windows on both sides of the car. (Missouri Pacific, Jim Bennett Collection)

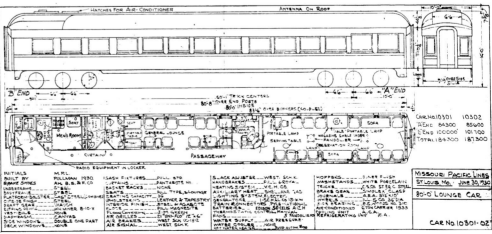

above: Car 760 was rebuilt as a grill-coach in 1963 and was renumbered to 561 within the year. The grill section featured both table and counter seating. The coach section contained 36 seats. (Missouri Pacific, Author's Collection)

left: No. 760 was originally a combination RPO-coach built for the *Delta Eagle*. It was later reassigned to the connecting train for the *Pioneer* between Harlingen and Mission, Texas. This photo of No. 760 was taken at Mission in 1955. (Ralph Carlson)

below: MoPac diner-lounge *Cheyenne Mountain* was built by Budd in 1942 for the new *Colorado Eagle*. The sister car was named *San Isabel*. The two served in diner-lounge service until 1963 when they were rebuilt to diner-parlors and renumbered from 742 to 36 and 743 to 37. (Missouri Pacific, Author's Collection)

top: This is how the *Colorado Eagle* diner lounge cars were configured after conversion to diner-parlor cars Nos. 36 and 37. (Missouri Pacific, Author's Collection)

Drawing specifications for Car No. 36-37:

BUILT BY	BUDD. LOT #9637
DATE BUILT	1942
UNDERFRAMING	STAINLESS STEEL
SUPERSTRUCTURE	" "
COUPLERS	TIGHTLOCK N.M.&S.CO.
DRAFT GEAR	WAUGHMAT
AIR BRAKES	WEST SCH. D-22-P
CONTROL VALVE	D-22-AR
BRAKE CYL.	12"x8" (2 PER TRUCK)
HANDBRAKE	NATIONAL 780

TRUCK BRAKES	ASF CO. CLASP
TRUCKS	CAST STEEL
WHEELS	36" DIA. ROLLED STL.
JOURNALS	5½"x10" LOUNGE END / 6"x11" KITCHEN END
ROLLER BRGS	TIMKEN
SHOCK ABSORBERS	MONROE #11503
SIDE BEARINGS	DREWS EVERITE
AIR CONDITIONING	MECHANICAL 8 TON
REFRIGERATING UNIT	8 TON FRIG.
COOLING UNIT	2-4 TON FRIG.

HEATING SYSTEM	VAPOR UNI-ZONE
AIR DISTRIBUTION	MULTI-VENT
LIGHTING	INCANDESCENT-KITCHEN / FLUORESCENT-DIN.&PARLOR
LIGHTING FIXTURES	SCH&L CO.
BATTERIES	64 VOLT
GENERATOR	35 KW SAFETY-BRL-3577S
GENEMOTOR DRIVE	SPICER
INSIDE FINISH	STEEL & FORMICA
FLOOR	1" PLYWOOD
FLOOR COVERING	BEIGE VINYL TILE

WINDOWS	HUNTER SASH
WINDOW GLASS	THERMOPANE UNITS
WINDOW SHADES	DODGE VENETIAN BLINDS
EXHAUST FANS	SAFETY & STURTEVANT
KITCHEN	STAINLESS STEEL
KITCHEN EQUIP'T.	ANGELO-COLONNA
RANGE & OIL BURNER	STEARNES
TABLES	BUDD MFG CO.
DINING ROOM UPH.	ROSE TAUPE
BRAKING POWER	

MISSOURI PACIFIC RAILROAD CO.
ST. LOUIS, MO.   SEPT. 6, 1963
DINER - PARLOR
CAR NO.-36-37

middle: Diner-lounges Nos. 42-44 were built by AC&F in 1948 for the Texas & Pacific *Eagle* service. The cars were originally numbered 525-527. (Missouri Pacific, Author's Collection)

DINER-LOUNGE   T&P.RY.CO.

KITCHEN VENTILATION — 2 AXIAL FLOW FANS MOD. L-2D, JOY. MFG. CO.

DATE	INT'L	CHANGE
8-13-63	LT	RENUMBERED FROM 525-527
8-15-57	B.E.	SPICER DRIVE & SPEED GOV'R LOCATED
9-16-54	B.R.	SUPERSEDES 15-15

SAME LOT AS MP 38-40

DATE BUILT	1948
BUILT BY A.C.& F CO.	LOT NO. 2880-A
BUILT AT	ST. CHARLES, MO.
UNDERFRAME	LOW ALLOY HIGH TENSILE STEEL
SUPERSTRUCTURE	ALUMINUM
COUPLERS	AAR TIGHTLOCK TYPE "H"
DRAFT GEAR	WAUGH EQUIPMENT CO'S
WAUGHMAT TWIN CUSHION TYPE WM-G-DF	
CENTER PINS	MINER SELF-LOCKING PINS

WATER SUPPLY	400 GALLONS
VENETIAN BLINDS	AJAX CO.S "DA-LITE"
GENEMOTOR-SCH&L CO's GP 25025, 25 KW	
BRAKE CYLINDER "UAHS" 4 (12" x 10")	
HAND BRAKE - MINER CO's VERTICAL WHEEL TYPE	
BRAKES-WESTINGHOUSE SCHEDULE "HSC"	
D-22-BR CONTROL VALVE, QUICK SERVICE VALVE	
21-B MAGNET F5-1864 RELAY VALVE	

WHEELS - 36" M.W. AAR CLASS "A", B-36	
JOURNALS - 6"x11" KITCHEN END; 5½"x10" DINING END (TIMKEN ROLLER BEARINGS)	
SHOCK ABSORBERS - HOUDE VERTICAL TYPE	
SPICER DRIVE - LOCATED AT BOXES 3 & 4	
AIR CONDITIONING - FRIGIDAIRE ELECTRO-MECHANICAL TYPE "EM"	
TRUCK BRAKE - SIMPLEX UNIT CYL. CLASP BRAKES	

HEATING - VAPOR CH. CO's THERMOSTATIC CONTROLLED ZONE SYSTEM OF HEAT.
BATTERIES - 32 CELLS, 16-2 CELL TRAYS 1000 AMP HOURS.

DINER-LOUNGE
CAR NO 42-44

bottom: MoPac invested heavily in combination types of equipment, such as grill-coaches, dormitory coaches, and dining-lounge cars. The *Eagle* combination fleet began with the purchase of two dining-bar-lounge cars for the two *Missouri River Eagle* trainsets. The bar-lounge area was decorated with a mural of a bald eagle in flight, in honor of the new trains' name. (Missouri Pacific, Author's Collection)

MISSOURI PACIFIC LINES
DINING AND LOUNGE CAR ROSTER (1963 RENUMBERING)

Railroad	Type	Series	Former Series	Notes		Railroad	Type	Series	Former Series	Notes
T&P	Diner	30	500			MP	Grill Coach	560	732	56 seats
MP	Diner	31	840			MP	Grill Coach	561	760	44 seats
MP	Dining Bar Lounge	34-35	740-741			MP	Grill Coach	562-563	761-762	32 seats
MP	Diner Lounge	36-37	742-743	50 seats		T&P	Grill Coach	569-570	480-481	53 seats
MP	Diner Lounge	38-40	843-845	50 seats		MP	Grill Coach	571-572	824-825	52 seats
T&P	Lounge	42-44	525-527	50 seats		MP	Diner Coach	580-581	841-842	
MP	Diner	70	10042	36 seats		MP	Diner Coach	582	847	
T&P	Diner	71-72	1018-1019			MP	Sleeper Lounge	640-642	Eagle Cliff Eagle Canyon Eagle Ridge	10 seats
T&P	Diner	73				MP	Grill Coach	1080	6408	
T&P	Diner	75				MP	Grill Coach	1081	6410	
MP	Diner Lounge	76	10047			MP	Grill Coach	1082	6413	
MP	Diner Lounge	77	10237	36 seats						
MP	Diner	78	10238							
MP	Diner Lounge	80	10402	32 seats						

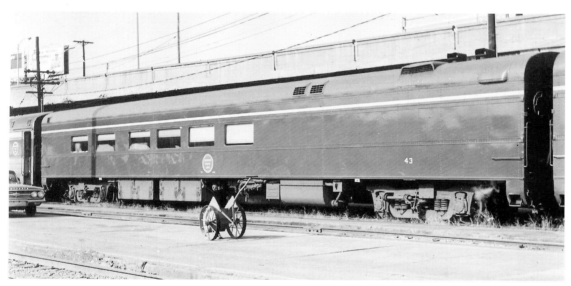

left: Texas & Pacific lounge car No. 43 illustrates the final blue scheme with the initials "TP" at the lower left side of the MoPac insignia.

below: MoPac No. 580 is actually a diner coach but has all the appearances of being a diner lounge (its configuration when built in 1948). The four windows to the right mark the coach section. (Both, William A. Raia Collection)

SLEEPING CARS

Sleeping cars are, without doubt, one of the finest means of travel. The Missouri Pacific operated a rather interesting fleet of standard heavyweight and streamlined Pullman sleeping cars throughout most of its history. Accommodations ranged from the standard upper and lower berths to compartments, bedrooms, drawing rooms, roomettes, and Slumbercoach rooms. The railroad also introduced the concept of the "Thrift-T-Sleeper" in which people traveling on coach fares paid only a supplementary accommodation charge for upper or lower berths. It was first-class travel on a coach ticket.

The photos and diagrams on the following pages illustrate the Missouri Pacific sleeping car fleet from the 1940s through the end of sleeping car service prior to Amtrak. What better way to enjoy an "eagle in flight" than in a Pullman sleeper on the *Texas* or *Colorado Eagles*?

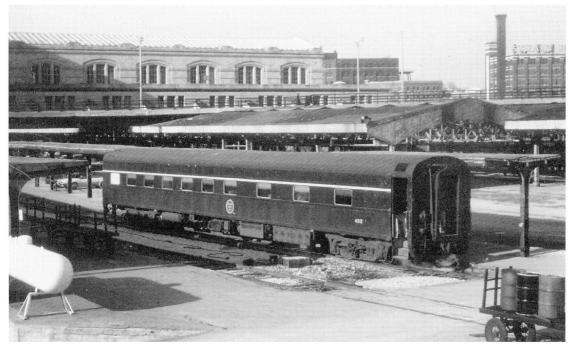

above: The *Texas Eagle* departs St. Louis Union Station and begins its westward trek. Behind the baggage car, coaches, dome, and portholed diner, two of the train's 14-roomette, 4-double bedroom sleeping cars are emerging from the station. (H. E. Williams, TLC Collection)

left: No. 402 is the former Pullman *Eagle Bridge*, a 14 roomette, 2 double bedroom, 1 drawing room sleeper. By the time of this January 1971 photo at Kansas City, the car had been rebuilt as a coach. (Ron Merrick)

above: Pullman 8-3-1 *Terminal Tower* operated over the MP. (Missouri Pacific, Author's Collection)

middle: Pullman 12-1 *Armington* was at Mission, Texas, in April 1949. (Ralph Carlson)

bottom: *Eagle Hill*, a 14-4, was built by P-S in 1948. (Missouri Pacific, Author's Collection)

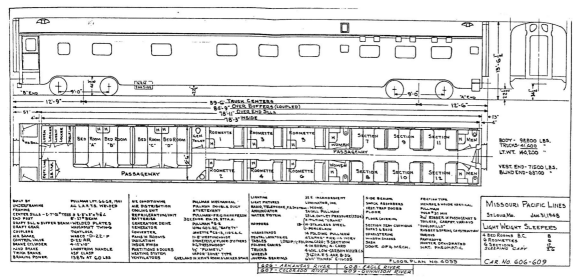

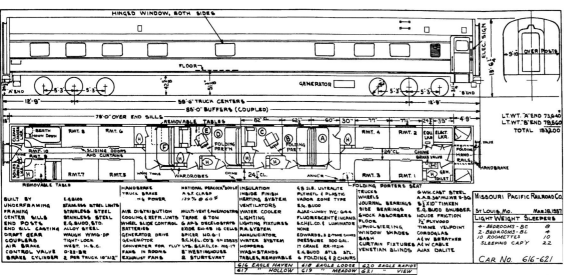

top: Missouri Pacific owned four 6 section, 6 roomette, and 4 double bedroom sleeping cars, series 606 to 609, built by P-S in 1941. (Missouri Pacific, Author's Collection)

middle: Diagram of the 616-621 series of 10 roomette, 6 double bedroom cars. (Missouri Pacific, Author's Collection)

bottom: *Eagle Hollow* was a 10-6 sleeper and part of series 616 to 621. Two things are intriguing about this series: the six-wheel trucks and the center placement of the double bedrooms with the roomettes at both ends of the car. (Jay Williams Collection)

EAGLE POOL CARS

upper right: Painted in MoPac *Eagle* colors, Pennsylvania Railroad 10-6 sleeper *Eagle Chief* operated in pooled through-car service between Texas and New York City. Note the small "PRR" initials in the upper corners. (Jay Williams Collection)

below: *Cascade Drive* was a Baltimore & Ohio car (note the "B&O" initials) operating in *Eagle* pool service between Washington, D.C. and Texas. The car was photographed at Cincinnati Union Terminal's coach yard in 1965.

opposite bottom: Another B&O 10-5 sleeper to wear MP *Eagle* colors was *Cascade Sound*, also at Cincinnati in January 1965. (Both, Julian Barnard, B&O Historical Society Collection)

Just as some Missouri Pacific *Eagle* equipment operated in through service to reach points on connecting railroads, a select few sleeping cars owned by other railroads were painted in *Eagle* colors as their contribution to pooled service.

The largest fleet of such cars over the years was owned by the Pennsylvania Railroad, and operated east of St. Louis to connect New York City and other important eastern centers with Texas points served by MoPac. Such through sleepers allowed passengers to occupy the same space for their entire journey, and not have to change cars en route. Instead, the through car they occupied was switched from train to train as required.

Eleven lightweight 10 roomette, 5 double bedroom cars built for PRR by Pullman-Standard in the summer of 1940 were painted in *Eagle* colors and assigned to the PRR-MP pool, as follows:

Cascade Bower	*Cascade Melody*
Cascade Cliff	*Cascade Peak*
Cascade Cove	*Cascade Pinnacle*
Cascade Crag	*Cascade Pool*
Cascade Hollow	*Cascade Slope*
Cascade Mantle	

As part of the Pennsylvania's postwar re-equipping, a like number of new AC&F 10 roomette, 6-double bedroom sleepers built in mid-1950 was painted in *Eagle* colors and assigned to the New York–Texas pool. These cars were:

Eagle Beam	*Eagle Eye*
Eagle Bluff	*Eagle Grand*
Eagle Charm	*Eagle Head*
Eagle Chief	*Eagle Oak*
Eagle Cove	*Eagle Park*
Eagle Pass	

Baltimore & Ohio entered a similar pooling arrangement with MoPac, but not to the degree of PRR's involvement. B&O assigned *Cascade*-series 10-5 sleepers to Washington, D.C.– Texas service, connecting at St. Louis from B&O's *National Limited* to MoPac's *Texas Eagle*. Two B&O 10-5s known to have worn *Eagle* colors were *Cascade Drive* and *Cascade Sound*, both built by P-S in 1942. In 1959, B&O acquired Budd Slumbercoaches *Restland*, *Sleepland*, and *Thriftland* for the pool.   —*Kevin J. Holland*

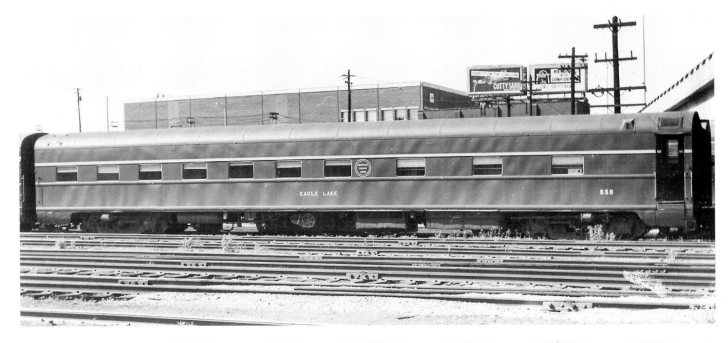

above: Missouri Pacific's *Eagle Lake*, a 14 roomette, 4 double bedroom car, after repainting in the simplified scheme with the MoPac insignia.

middle: *Eagle Island*, another 14-4 car, illustrates the opposite side and second-last paint/insignia scheme for the Texas & Pacific. Note the T&P diamond applied between the roomette and bedroom windows.

bottom: Texas & Pacific No. 624, *Eagle Domain*, a 10-6 car, illustrates the last T&P livery, with the "TP" initials at the lower left of the insignia. (Three photos, William A. Raia Collection)

opposite: Slumbercoach *Southland* began operating in Washington–Texas service with the B&O in 1959. *Southland* was sold to the Northern Pacific in 1964. The car had one of the shortest careers of any type of passenger car on the Missouri Pacific. (Missouri Pacific, Author's Collection)

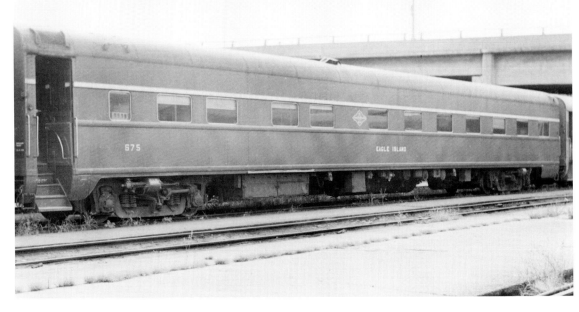

MISSOURI PACIFIC LINES
SLEEPING CAR ROSTER (1963 RENUMBERING)

Railroad	Type	No.	Former Name	Notes
MP	6-6-4	606	*Arkansas River*	
		607	*Colorado River*	
		608	*Eagle River*	
		609	*Gunnison River*	
MP	10-6	610	*Canyon River*	
		611	*Crystal River*	
		612	*Elk River*	
		613	*Roaring River*	
		614	*Eagle Butte*	
		615	*Eagle Chasm*	
		616	*Eagle Haven*	
		617	*Eagle Hollow*	
		618	*Eagle Lodge*	
		619	*Eagle Meadow*	
		620	*Eagle Rapids*	
		621	*Eagle View*	
T&P	10-6	622	*Eagle Brook*	
		623	*Eagle County*	
		624	*Eagle Domain*	
		625	*Eagle Path*	
MP	14-2-1	630	*Eagle Bridge*	
		631	*Eagle Circle*	
		632	*Eagle Country*	
		633	*Eagle Glide*	
		634	*Eagle Village*	
T&P	14-2-1	635	*Eagle Flight*	
MP	5-Lounge	640	*Eagle Cliff*	(Listed in Chapter 9)
		641	*Eagle Canyon*	
		642	*Eagle Ridge*	
MP	14-4	650	*Eagle Chain*	
		651	*Eagle Creek*	
		652	*Eagle Crest*	
		653	*Eagle Dam*	
		654	*Eagle Divide*	
		655	*Eagle Forest*	
		656	*Eagle Height*	
		657	*Eagle Hill*	
		658	*Eagle Knob*	
		659	*Eagle Lake*	
		660	*Eagle Mountain*	
		661	*Eagle Point*	
		662	*Eagle Preserve*	
		663	*Eagle Refuge*	
		664	*Eagle Rock*	
		665	*Eagle Stream*	
		666	*Eagle Summit*	
		667	*Eagle Tree*	
		668	*Eagle Turn*	
		669	*Eagle Valley*	
		670	*Eagle Woods*	
T&P	14-4	671	*Eagle Bay*	
		672	*Eagle Beach*	
		673	*Eagle Call*	
		674	*Eagle City*	
		675	*Eagle Island*	
		676	*Eagle Land*	
		677	*Eagle Light*	
		678	*Eagle Rest*	
		679	*Eagle Road*	
		680	*Eagle Spirit*	
		681	*Eagle Trail*	
		682	*Eagle Watch*	
MP	8-5	684	*Clover Spray*	
		685	*Ixtacchautl*	
		686	*Sierra Madre*	
		687	*Malinche*	
MP	8-3-1	690	*Thrift-T-1*	
		691	*Thrift-T-2*	
		693	*Thrift-T-3*	
MP	24-8	699	*Southland*	Slumbercoach

Sleeping Car Designations:

6-6-4	6 roomettes, 6 sections, 4 double bedrooms
10-6	10 roomettes, 6 double bedrooms
14-2-1	14 roomettes, 2 double bedrooms, 1 drawing room
5-L	5 double bedrooms, lounge
14-4	14 roomette, 4 double bedrooms
8-5	8 sections, 5 double bedrooms
8-3-1	8 sections, 3 double bedrooms, 1 drawing room
10-2-1	10 sections, 2 compartments, 1 drawing room
12-1	12 sections, 1 drawing room
8-2-1	8 sections, 2 compartments, 1 drawing room
4-4-5-1	4 sections, 4 roomettes, 5 double bedrooms, 1 compartment
24-8	Slumbercoach, 24 single rooms, 8 double rooms

BUSINESS CARS

The Missouri Pacific's business car fleet has existed and evolved from the earliest days of the many lines that made up the MoPac system. Following merger with the Union Pacific, former MoPac business cars carried the yellow UP colors with MISSOURI PACIFIC lettering. This chapter reviews the MoPac fleet during the last half-century, from the blue and light gray, the solid blue, and finally, the UP colors.

Business cars most often operated on the rear of various trains. With their open end observation platforms, the cars were a perfect "punctuation" for the passenger train (even though they were not open to regular passengers). The primary purpose of the cars included inspection tours, shippers' specials, directors' specials, and various other events. The latter included charter trips, conveying politicians from the United States and many other countries, and even funerals of dignitaries.

The business cars' primary use, however, was serving the company managers touring the railroad and holding meetings at various locations. If the meetings were small enough, they could be held in the dining room or the observation room of the car. In later years, the business cars were sometimes attached to Amtrak trains, but freight trains were the dominant carrier for one- or two-car movements. Other movements included trains known as "Business Car Specials," again, the purpose being tours of the railroad for the company's managers, directors, and shippers. Sometimes one would find business cars from other railroads traveling over the line while looking over the possibility of through freight train schedules, potential mergers, and a whole host of other corporate objectives.

Still another component of company service equipment included classroom or instruction cars.

In many cases, various types of obsolete passenger cars were rebuilt with new interiors and major changes in the exterior window arrangements for the cars' next step in their careers. In fact, sometimes, the changes were so extensive that few could tell what the original car might have been by simply looking at the car.

The instruction or classroom cars were handled in all types of trains, including business car trains where the cars were used as full meeting rooms during the travel time. In order to match its passenger trains, the MoPac painted these cars in the passenger color schemes of the particular era. And like the business cars, the equipment continued in service with the most up-to-date MoPac color schemes from the beginning of Amtrak until complete inclusion in the Union Pacific system. Thus, MoPac passenger cars continued to thrive, in some way, beyond May 1971.

above: Business car No. 12 was rebuilt in 1957 as car No. 1. This photo illustrates the bedroom side of No. 1. It was the last car of a 14-car special train en route from Omaha to New Orleans in December 1980. (Jim Bennett)

above: MoPac Air Brake Instruction car No. 60. (Missouri Pacific, Author's Collection)

middle: Business car No. 1, prior to the 1957 reconstruction of No. 12 and its subsequent renumbering to No. 1. This earlier No. 1 was at Harlingen, Texas, in March 1955. (Ralph Carlson)

below: No. 12 emerged as the new No. 1 in January 1957, complete with the name *Eagle*. (AC&F, Kevin J. Holland Collection)

MISSOURI PACIFIC LINES BUSINESS CAR ROSTER (1963 RENUMBERING)

Railroad	Type	No.	Former No.	Notes
MP	Business	1	12	
MP	Business	2	2	
MP	Business	3	3	
MP	Business	4	4	
MP	Business	6	6	
MP	Business	7	7	
MP	Business	8	8	
T&P	Business	9	1	
MP	Business	10		
MP	Sleeper-Lounge	11	611	Former 10-6 sleeper *Crystal River*
MP	Air Brake Instruction	20	465	
MP	Instruction	21	6126	
T&P	Instruction	23	1603	
T&P	Heater	25-27	50-52	
MP	Fuel Instruction	65	6122	

Here are two views of No. 12 prior to its 1957 reconstruction by AC&F as No. 1. In the *Eagle* paint scheme the car carried the full "Missouri Pacific Lines" name with the initials "M.P." in the corners and "M.P. 12" above the door on the rear platform. (Both, Missouri Pacific, Author's Collection)

right: Diagram for new No. 1 (old No. 12). (Jim Bennett Collection)

middle: Business car No. 8, with stainless steel platform, at St. Louis in 1970. (William A. Raia Collection)

bottom: Texas & Pacific No. 9. Dressed in the MoPac blue, the T&P's initials are located just to the left of the insignia. (Jay Williams Collection)

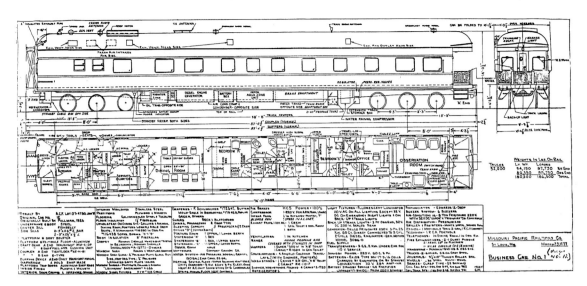

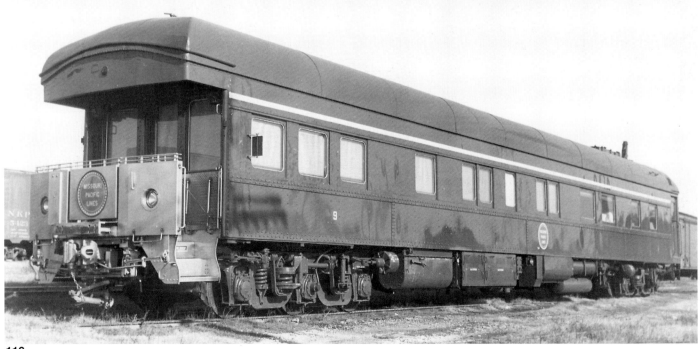

top: MoPac business car No. 2 was at St. Louis in 1967. (Jay Williams Collection)

second from top: Instruction car No. 20 was rebuilt from Budd coach No. 465 and has lost its lower side fluting. The car was photographed in service at Harlingen, Texas, in February 1974. (Ralph Carlson)

second from bottom: Missouri Pacific converted a full sleeping car for business train services. No. 11 is a former 10 roomette, 6 double bedroom car with a new configuration of 6 bedrooms, 3 roomettes and center car lounge. The sleeping rooms can accommodate 15 passengers, while the lounge area seats 18. There was no immediate change in the car's window configuration. (William A. Raia Collection)

below: Business car *St. Louis* was formerly MP No. 1. This view in Union Pacific colors was taken in 1984, after MoPac's merger into the UP system. (Camille Chappuis)

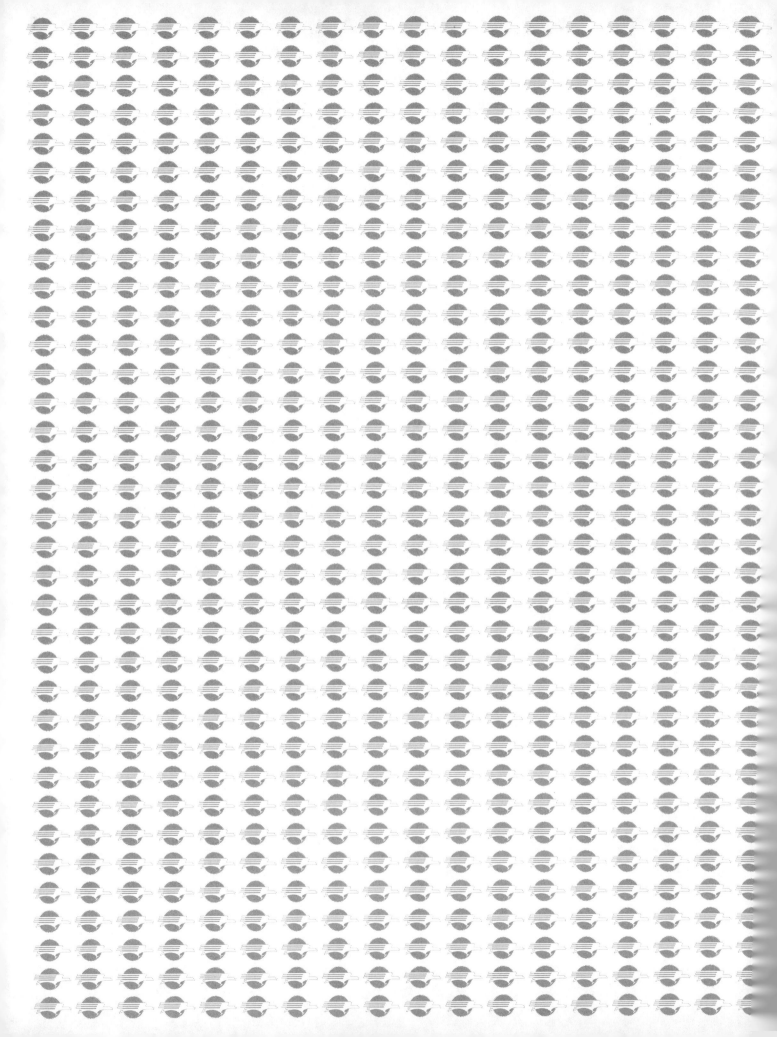